WHO OWNS THE PRESS?

WHO OWNS THE PRESS?

Investigating Public vs. Private Ownership of America's Newspapers

MARY JANE PARDUE

Marion Street Press
Portland, Oregon

Published by Marion Street Press
4207 SE Woodstock Blvd # 168
Portland, OR 97206-6267
USA
http://www.marionstreetpress.com/

Orders and desk copies: (800) 888-4741

Printed in the United States of America

ISBN 978-1-933338-30-9

Cover art direction by Nicky Ip
Back cover photo by John Wall

See pages *ix–x* for copyright permissions.

Library of Congress Cataloging-in-Publication Data

Pardue, Mary Jane, 1949-
 Who owns the press? : investigating public vs. private ownership of America's
newspapers / by Mary Jane Pardue.
    p. cm.
 Includes bibliographical references and index.
 ISBN 978-1-933338-30-9
 1. American newspapers--Ownership--Economic aspects--History--21st century.
 2. Newspaper publishing--Economic aspects--United States--History--21st century.
 3. Journalism--Economic aspects--United States--History--21st century. 4. American
newspapers--Objectivity. 5. Press monopolies--United States--History--21st century. I.
Title.
 PN4888.O85P37 2010
 338.4'30713--dc22

                                      2010031159

To Victor, who showed me the value of positive thinking

Contents

Acknowledgments

With any book, support for the author can make a lengthy and difficult process bearable and ultimately self-fulfilling. My experience was no different. I was fortunate to have the strong support of my friends and colleagues at Missouri State University as well as many students and others who showed strong interest throughout the process. There are some to whom I would like to offer special thanks.

First, I would like to thank Philip Meyer, Knight chair and professor emeritus of journalism at the University of North Carolina at Chapel Hill. Professor Meyer's book *The Vanishing Newspaper* inspired me to explore how family owned newspapers are fundamentally different from publicly owned ones. I want to thank Professor Meyer for helping me find a way to fund transcription services and expensive travel across the country, from the Pacific Northwest to the newspapers in New England, down South, and across the Midwest. But most importantly, he gave me this advice on more than one occasion: "Keep minimizing the space between your nose and the grindstone." It proved to be the best advice I could have received.

I would like to thank John Mennenga, facilitator of the Independent Newspaper Group (ING), for generously sharing financial benchmarking data of ING papers and his analyses. He offered valuable expertise and opinions on the state of the industry as well as the economic future of newspapers.

I would like to thank my former editor and publisher, Ed Avis of Marion Street Press, who helped me see the bigger picture for this book. His suggestions showed me how to turn what would have been simply an academic exercise into a project that has broader appeal and value not only to those studying newspapers but also to those who work at and own them.

I also would like to thank Kel Winter and Jim Schuette, who bought Marion Street Press in 2009 and immediately realized the timeliness and value of this project. They offered a fresh perspective and expert advice and worked tirelessly to help me finish it.

Special thanks go to the publishers and managers at the eight newspapers I visited for their time and interest in this project. They welcomed me into their newspapers, willingly provided information, and made key staff members available during my visits. They brought me up to speed on the latest techniques and operations in the departments at their newspapers. They aggressively tested my thesis, candidly answered all my questions, and challenged me to reexamine my conclusions.

Finally, I would like to thank my family who checked on me regularly with the simple question: "How's the book coming?" and the hope for a positive response. I owe special appreciation to my nephew Victor for his help and encouragement, which I find impossible to fully acknowledge.

—Mary Jane Pardue

Arkansas Democrat-Gazette interviews with Walter Hussman, Paul Smith, Philip S. Anderson, Lynn Hamilton. Used with permission.

Arkansas Gazette Company v. Camden News Publishing Company, No. LR C 84 1020 (E.D. Ark. 1986), Defendant's Trial Exhibit # 548. Used with permission.

Arkansas Gazette Company v. Camden News Publishing Company, No. LR C 84 1020 (E.D. Ark. 1986), Defendant's Trial Exhibit # 596. Used with permission.

Lynn Hamilton (vice president of operations, *Arkansas Democrat-Gazette*) to author, memorandum, 28 Oct. 2003. Used with permission.

Anniston Star interviews with H. Brandt Ayers, Chris Waddle, Ed Fowler, Phillip A. Sanguinetti, Troy Turner, Bob Davis, Robert Jackson II, Dennis Dunn. Used with permission.

Anniston Star, About Us, http://www.annisonstar.com/. Used with permission.

Spokesman-Review interviews with Stacey Cowles, Robert Davis, Paul Schafer, Steve Smith, Daniel Johnson, Shaun O'L. Higgins. Used with permission.

Register-Guard interviews with Tony Baker, Fletcher Little, Dave Baker, Jerry LaCamp, Charles Downing. Used with permission.

Welch, Bob. "R-G owners celebrate 75 years." *Register-Guard*, March 3, 2002. Used with permission.

Concord Monitor interviews with Geordie Wilson, Tom Brown, Mike Pride, Felice Belman, Ann-Marie Forrester, David Hanks. Used with permission.

Daily Hampshire Gazette interviews with Aaron Julien, Peter DeRose, Jim Foudy, Mark Elliott, Priscilla Flynn, Dennis Skoglund. Used with permission.

Tulsa World interviews with Robert E. Lorton III, Steve Barlow, Joe Worley, Bill King, Bill Carr. Used with permission.

The *Gazette in Cedar Rapids* interviews with Joe Hladky, Peg Schmitz, Chuck Peters, Elizabeth Hladky, Mark Bowden, Scott Swenson. Used with permission.

Excerpts from Hladky, Joe. *The Enduring Vision: The Gazette Co.* (Cedar Rapids: Gazette Co., 2005). Used with permission.

John Mennenga (Independent Newspaper Group), interview with the author. Used with permission.

John Mennenga, "ING Financial Benchmarking, Fiscal Year 2005, based on Inland Press Cost and Revenue Study" (PowerPoint presentation, Independent Newspaper Group, Kansas City, MO, fall 2005). Used with permission.

John Mennenga, "ING Circulation" (info sheet on 2006 circulation of ING newspapers, Independent Newspaper Group, Kansas City, MO, fall 2005). Used with permission.

Pardue, Mary Jane. "Quality Key to Highest City Zone Penetration in U.S.," *Newspaper Research Journal* 25, no. 4 (fall 2004): 13–25. Used with permission.

The Pew Research Center's Project for Excellence in Journalism, The State of the News Media 2007, March 12, 2007, http://www.stateofthemedia.org/2007. Used with permission.

The Pew Research Center's Project for Excellence in Journalism, The State of the News Media 2009, March 16, 2009, http://www.stateofthemedia.org/2009/index.htm/. Used with permission.

Max Brantley, interview by Ernest Dumas, Feb. 25, 2000, Arkansas Gazette Project, Pryor Center for Arkansas Oral and Visual History, Special Collections, University of Arkansas Libraries, Fayetteville.
URL: http://libinfo.uark.edu/SpecialCollections/ACOVH/default.asp (accessed July 27, 2004). Used with permission.

Jack Meriwether, interview by Ernest Dumas and Roy Reed, Nov. 28, 2000, Arkansas Gazette Project, Pryor Center for Arkansas Oral and Visual History, Special Collections, University of Arkansas Libraries, Fayetteville.
URL: http://libinfo.uark.edu/SpecialCollections/ACOVH/default.asp (accessed July 27, 2004). Used with permission.

Ernest Dumas, interview by Roy Reed, Oct. 24, 2000, Arkansas Gazette Project, Pryor Center for Arkansas Oral and Visual History, Special Collections, University of Arkansas Libraries, Fayetteville.
URL: http://libinfo.uark.edu/SpecialCollections/ACOVH/default.asp (accessed July 27, 2004). Used with permission.

Preface

When you step into the *Arkansas Democrat-Gazette* in Little Rock; the *Anniston Star* in Anniston, Alabama; or the *Register-Guard* in Eugene, Oregon, you feel like you're in any other newspaper in the country at the dawn of the twenty-first century. You'll likely see newspapers and reports stacked high on desks, half-filled coffee cups, or the remains of lunch, as writers and editors work to make sense of the news of the day. As the clock ticks relentlessly overhead, reporters dig their way through a morass of information, find people to interview, and write their stories to post on the newspaper's website and for the next day's print edition. It's a heartening scene—journalists driven by a higher calling to fulfill their role in American democracy, knowing that despite long workdays and daunting tasks, their communities depend on them to serve as information providers, civic watchdogs, and independent monitors of power. Their goal is always the same—to keep their readers informed and to help them make good decisions.

But as journalists toil at newspapers across the nation, pursuing daily stories of government, business, and local citizens, they themselves have become a big story. Newspapers today are endangered—many not by an external force but by a more menacing internal one: their owners. Fifty years ago, most newspapers in the United States were locally owned. Today, many are owned by media conglomerates for which shareholder return trumps the principles of journalism.

Newspapers have evolved into a mature industry whose future, some believe, is in jeopardy. The evidence is mounting. Circulation has declined along with advertising revenues. Changing reader habits and the emergence of new technologies have driven many readers, especially younger ones, away from newspapers to other sources of news. The effect on newspaper companies is devastating.

A particularly troubling year was 2006, which brought the sale and breakup of Knight Ridder, formerly the second largest newspaper chain and considered by many experts to be among the best. Private Capital Management, an investment group led by Bruce S. Sherman, forced Knight Ridder to sell itself to the McClatchy Company in a $4.5 billion deal that included thirty-two daily newspapers with circulation totaling 3.7 million. The reason? Disappointment with Knight Ridder's poor stock performance. McClatchy immediately announced the sale of twelve of the papers.[1] The news delivered a devastating blow to the industry. The *New York Times* quoted former Knight Ridder Publisher Jay T. Harris in an August 2006 article saying: "Could anyone imagine 10 years ago saying that in 10 years, Knight Ridder would not exist? It was one of the strongest newspaper companies in America. How could you have a hand like that and play it in such a way that you would end up losing everything?"[2]

The answer lies in changes in newspaper ownership. Fifty years ago families owned most of the daily newspapers in the country. But as new production technologies developed, the industry was transformed and newspapers thrived financially. As a result, they became attractive investments. Companies went public to raise funds to grow, and a widespread media consolidation in the last decades of the twentieth century left four out of five daily newspapers controlled by major corporations, or "chains."[3] The focus of newspaper owners shifted, however, when companies became publicly owned.

As 2006 drew to a close, the U.S. economy was showing signs of strengthening. The Dow Jones Industrial Average closed over 12,000 for the first time on October 19, and finished out the year on December 27 at 12,510.57. The trend continued in 2007 when the Dow closed at a high of 14,000.41 on July 19, up 12.3 percent for the year.[4] The financial health of American business looked good, with corporate profits on the rise. But at U.S. newspapers, the picture remained bleak. Profits were on the skids virtually across the board. The slide in ad sales, exacerbated by a softening real estate market and higher oil prices, continued along with rising costs and the threat of emerging technologies.

At the beginning of 2006, the industry had about three thousand fewer full-time newsroom employees than in 2000, as owners tried to slash their way to profit. Reduced news hole, or the space on a page filled with news rather than ads, and smaller newspapers with a greater local focus marked the industry.[5] But as the economy retracted at the end of 2007, the United States began slipping into a deep recession, which meant more bad news for newspapers. When the Project for Excellence in Journalism (PEJ) released its sixth—and bleakest—annual report on the State of the News Media* in the United States

---

* "The State of the News Media is the work of the Project for Excellence in Journalism, a nonpolitical, nonpartisan research institute that is part of the Pew Research Center in Washington. The study was funded by the Pew Charitable Trusts" (The Pew Research Center's Project for Excellence in Journalism, The State of the News Media 2010, "Preface," http://www.stateofthemedia.org/2010).

in 2009, it reported that newspaper ad revenue had declined 23 percent in the previous two years. "Some newspapers are in bankruptcy, and others have lost three-quarters of their value. By our calculations, nearly one out of every five journalists working for newspapers in 2001 is now gone ..."[6]

Looking back, the Knight Ridder sale had dropped a reality check on a languishing industry. And it didn't stop with Knight Ridder. Two more deals shocked newspapers in 2007. The first came in April when real estate mogul Sam Zell won a bid for the Tribune Company in a complicated $8.2 billion deal that involved taking the company private, paying shareholders thirty-four dollars a share, and creating an employee stock ownership plan. Tribune had a tough year in 2006 with a flat stock price, disgruntled stockholders, and internal struggles at its newspapers. The company was considering its options "to maximize shareholder value," said CEO Dennis J. FitzSimons.[7] While few industry insiders were surprised that the company took action, the deal attracted substantial attention because of its buyer and his creative financing.

But perhaps the most unsettling transaction to industry watchers was the July 2007 sale of Dow Jones, owner of the *Wall Street Journal*, to Rupert Murdoch, owner of News Corporation, for $5 billion.[8] While the Bancrofts, Dow Jones' owners for one hundred years, should be credited with taking steps during acquisition talks to preserve the independent voice of the *Journal*, the family ultimately became the poster child for what can happen to a family owned company when members disagree. Complicating matters was the fact that the company in recent years had faced the same struggles as other newspaper companies.

It is with these events in mind that a look at the differences in newspaper ownership models is warranted. Specifically it's important when attempting to assess newspapers' future to compare public and private ownership to see what factors drive each type. Those factors naturally lie at the heart of a company's business strategy and daily operations. It should be noted, however, that the state of American newspapers is continually changing, and any analysis must focus on one point in time.

The Numbers

There were 1,437 daily newspapers in 2006, according to the Newspaper Association of America, compared to 1,878 in 1940.[9] In its 2009 report, PEJ said the number of daily newspapers was down for the fourth straight year. There were 1,422 daily newspapers in 2007, down from 1,437 in 2006. The number of evening papers dropped by forty-nine in 2007, compared to a decline of thirty-one from 2005 to 2006.[10]

By October 2009 when the Audit Bureau of Circulations (ABC) released daily circulation figures for the six months ending in September, the *Wall Street Journal* had eclipsed *USA TODAY* and moved into first place. The top five newspapers, according to ABC, were:

- The *Wall Street Journal*—2,024,269
- *USA TODAY*—1,900,116
- The *New York Times*—927,851
- The *Los Angeles Times*—657,467
- The *Washington Post*—582,844.[11]

Of the top five, all showed declines from the same period in 2008 except for the *Journal*, which marked a 0.61 percent increase. The *Chicago Tribune* dropped to eighth place with 465,892 behind the New York *Daily News* with 544,167 and the *New York Post* with 508,042. Finishing out the top ten were the *Houston Chronicle* with 384,419 and the *Philadelphia Inquirer* with 361,480.[12]

As the recession deepened in 2008, the market for newspaper purchases dried up. PEJ noted that while plenty of newspapers were for sale at bargain prices, there were no buyers because there was no assurance that ad revenues would improve with an economic rebound or that new owners had any clear plans for how to regain profitability if they bought a newspaper. Complicating matters were tight credit markets for business expansion in a recession. The future was just as bleak. "Newspaper stocks, which had lost 42 percent of their value from the start of 2005 to the end of 2007, lost an astonishing 83 percent of their remaining value during 2008," PEJ reported in 2009.[13]

Relentless chain building can be blamed in part for the financial state public newspaper companies find themselves in today. Ten of the largest public newspaper companies dove into the wild years of expansion that swept the industry in the 1990s. The Project on the State of the American Newspaper followed newspaper sales between January 1994 and July 2000 and counted 719 transactions, noting that, "In over one hundred cases, a newspaper changed hands two, three or even four times in that brief period."[14] The buying and selling spree continued well after the turn of the century.

Many newspaper companies, like other companies needing money to grow, were lured to initial public offerings. For years, strong earnings meant consistently high stock prices. The rules change, though, when a company goes public, something newspapers realized perhaps late in the game as their economic model weakened. Publicly owned companies operate decidedly differently from privately owned ones.

The primary goal of a publicly owned company is a healthy financial return for shareholders. And even if the company is owned by a private equity group, it often behaves much like a publicly owned company. Family owned newspapers also seek profits, of course, but have different priorities. There are alternative ownership models, such as nonprofit foundations and employee stock ownership plans, which often put journalism ahead of profits. But they are not widely used.

The family owned newspaper model is perhaps the most viable model today because families make their own rules. Family ownership does not guarantee more financial stability or even a better journalistic product. Family owners can impose as strict financial goals as their public counterparts do. And family owners can be in business solely to make money or for the public exposure that comes with owning a city's newspaper. But there is a stability present at family owned newspapers that is less common at publicly owned ones.

To explore the differences between publicly owned and privately owned newspaper companies, I studied eight family owned newspapers across the country to examine their daily operations and to see if private ownership put them at an advantage to survive the challenges all newspapers face today. The newspapers are: *Arkansas Democrat-Gazette* in Little Rock, Arkansas; the *Anniston-Star* in Anniston, Alabama; the *Spokesman-Review* in Spokane, Washington; the *Register-Guard* in Eugene, Oregon; *Concord Monitor* in Concord, New Hampshire; *Daily Hampshire Gazette* in Northampton, Massachusetts; *Tulsa World* in Tulsa, Oklahoma; and the *Gazette* in Cedar Rapids, Iowa.

These newspapers were chosen to represent family owned newspapers of different sizes and in different regions of the country. They also represent variations on family ownership, including a foundation and a type of employee ownership. The story of each newspaper is presented as a case study based on interviews with the publishers and key managers who describe the newspapers' values and daily operations. The eight newspapers, while all different, represent how family owned papers are typically run in today's era of corporate journalism.

Notes

1 Katharine Q. Seelye, "What-Ifs of a Media Eclipse," *New York Times*, Aug. 27, 2006.
2 Ibid.
3 Melvin Mencher, *News Reporting and Writing* (New York: McGraw-Hill, 2011), 69.
4 Vikas Bajaj, "Dow Caps a 4-Month Surge, Closing Above 14,000," *New York Times*, July 20, 2007.
5 The Pew Research Center's Project for Excellence in Journalism, The State of the News Media 2007, http://www.stateofthemedia.org/2007/narrative_newspapers_newsinvestment.asp?cat=5&media=3.
6 The Pew Research Center's Project for Excellence in Journalism, The State of the News Media 2009, http://www.stateofthemedia.org/2009/narrative_overview_intro.php?media=1.

7 Katharine Q. Seelye and Andrew Ross Sorkin, "Tribune Quietly Opens Door to Sale of Individual Assets," *New York Times*, Nov. 2, 2006.

8 Richard Perez-Pena and Andrew Ross Sorkin, "Dow Jones Deal Gives Murdoch A Coveted Prize," *New York Times*, Aug. 1, 2007.

9 Newspaper Association of America, "Total Paid Circulation," http://www.naa.org/TrendsandNumbers/Total-Paid-Circulation.aspx.

10 The Pew Research Center's Project for Excellence in Journalism, The State of the News Media 2009, http://www.stateofthemedia.org/2009/narrative_newspapers_audience.php?media=4&cat=2.

11 *Editor & Publisher*, "Top 25 Daily Newspapers in New FAS-FAX," *Editor & Publisher*, http://www.editorandpublisher.com/Headlines/top-25-daily-newspapers-in-new-fas-fax-27476-.aspx (Oct. 27, 2009).

12 Ibid.

13 The Pew Research Center's Project for Excellence in Journalism, The State of the News Media 2009, http://www.stateofthemedia.org/2009/narrative_newspapers_ownership.php?media=4&cat=5.

14 Gene Roberts, ed., *Leaving Readers Behind: The Age of Corporate Newspapering* (Fayetteville: University of Arkansas Press, 2001), 51.

PART
ONE

The Family Newspaper Ownership Model

Simply put, the fundamental difference between family owned newspapers and publicly owned ones is that they play by different rules. In fact, family owned newspapers set their own rules. They can choose quality over profit or vice versa. They can take years to make crucial decisions, or they can seize opportunities as they arise to maximize returns. They can focus on long-term strategies or short-term results—and they can shift from one strategy to another from year to year or even quarter to quarter. They can and are often willing to accept lower profits if they choose, without answering to outside owners and Wall Street who demand consistently higher returns for their investment. They have fewer owners to please and complete control over their company finances, which is a huge decision-making advantage.

Family owned newspapers were often founded by owners who created successful businesses out of decades of toil and personal sacrifice. They hold dear what they consider the sacred purpose of journalism and believe their newspapers are a public trust. Many owners were journalists first, called to a profession and bound by basic values etched into their consciousness.

The purpose of journalism that guides family owned newspapers is best described by Bill Kovach and Tom Rosenstiel in *The Elements of Journalism*: "To provide citizens with the information they need to be free and self-governing." Kovach and Rosenstiel set forth the following principles to lead journalists:

- Journalism's first obligation is to the truth.
- Its first loyalty is to citizens.
- Its essence is a discipline of verification.
- Its practitioners must maintain an independence from those they cover.
- It must serve as an independent monitor of power.
- It must provide a forum for public criticism and compromise.

- It must strive to make the significant interesting and relevant.
- It must keep the news comprehensive and proportional.
- Its practitioners must be allowed to exercise their personal conscience.*

To be sure, profit seeking, influence peddling, and personal agendas have driven some family owned newspaper publishers. Public companies put a priority on providing high shareholder value, and private firms that buy newspapers solely as investments with plans to flip the properties as soon as their financial goals are realized aren't so concerned about the journalistic mission of the profession either. But for many of the family owned newspapers that have survived, there is an undeniable pride in their legacy and closer ties to their communities.

Ultimately, however, it is the owners' fundamental focus—or the top priority of the publisher—that sets family owned newspapers apart from publicly owned ones. Certainly family newspapers have stockholders to whom they are financially accountable, and they must make money to stay in business. They, too, are facing the same daunting challenges that all newspapers are facing today. But at family owned newspapers, the emphasis is usually twofold— financial results and quality journalism—and not necessarily in that order.

The Positives

Family owned newspapers share some positive characteristics that better position them to succeed in the changing environment newspapers find themselves today. They are:

- Functional autonomy—the ability to set their own agendas independently with a focus on long-range plans over short-term financial results.
- Streamlined operations—the ability to make quick decisions about their business and news coverage through fewer layers of management.
- Not driven by Wall Street—being accountable to a smaller group of stockholders who usually are related to one another.
- Long-term business relationships—strong ties to local advertisers and other family businesses.
- Strong family pride—a sense of tradition, appreciation of their family legacy, deep roots in the community, and an inherent understanding of the newspaper's role in their community.
- More control over their numbers—the ability to adjust ad rates, newspaper prices, profit margins, and staff size without approval from distant corporate bosses.

---

* Bill Kovach and Tom Rosenstiel, *The Elements of Journalism* (New York: Three Rivers Press, 2001), 17.

• Stronger and more loyal readership—closer ties to their community and readers who feel a sense of ownership and trust in their hometown newspaper.

The eight newspapers in the case studies that follow in Part Two demonstrate these seven positive characteristics. In every case, the publishers and top managers said the focus on long-term results was the biggest advantage of being family owned. They compared their operations with public newspaper companies and noted the fundamental differences long-term thinking makes every day. In many cases, managers also had worked for public newspaper companies, and all of them said they felt better about what they were doing at a family owned newspaper. While some public newspaper chains tout local autonomy for their individual newspapers, there is still an underlying one-size-fits-all mentality aimed at continuities and efficiencies that drives the company. As the company goes, so go the decisions at every newspaper, many times regardless of individual newspapers' needs and successes.

In every case study, the family owned newspaper managers noted the ease with which decisions are made and the fewer layers of bureaucracy that exist at their companies. There are simply not as many people running the show. Having a publisher with decision-making authority in the same building makes a huge difference when it comes to efficiency, problem solving, and seizing business opportunities. The managers noted that they don't have to file redundant reports with countless executives at distant headquarters, only to be told unexpectedly that the company's direction has changed. The ultimate decider when it comes to spending money at publicly owned newspapers is usually not the local publisher but an executive at headquarters who is making decisions in a far bigger context. One newspaper is only a unit—a single cost center—of the larger public company. Thus, decisions are made with an eye toward the impact spending will have on other properties, the company at large, and ultimately shareholder value. If one newspaper's capital needs are too great, for instance, or can be seen as detrimental to the company's financial performance, which can be assessed as often as weekly, the company may choose to delay capital improvements or simply to sell the property.

Decisions at public companies are made within the framework of Wall Street's expectations for the company's quarterly financial results. Money managers have less regard for the effect their decisions will have on journalism and more concern with the company's bottom line. At a family owned newspaper where the publisher rose through the editorial ranks, decisions are always made with at least an awareness of how they impact the quality of the newspaper's journalism. That's not to say that all decisions are driven by journalistic values. There is, however, usually an appreciation of those values if a publisher who also is a journalist makes the decisions.

The publishers at the family owned newspapers tend to have been in their jobs or at least at the newspaper for many years. They frequently are the descendants of previous publishers and grew up learning about the newspaper over the family dinner table. They know a number of people in the community and are accessible. Local advertisers feel free to walk into their office with comments or concerns, and they are recognized wherever they go.

At public newspaper companies, publishers often are on a two- or three-year cycle. They are assigned to one town, work hard to prove themselves—which really means improving the financial performance of the newspaper—then promoted on to the next larger market where the cycle is repeated. They sometimes end up at corporate headquarters making decisions for other publishers in the field. The results of revolving-door publishers are often little understanding of the real issues in a local community and a lack of personal interest in that community. In contrast, the publishers in the case studies have a high degree of understanding of local issues and are driven by a sincere personal interest in their communities. People often hate to see family businesses fold or sell out to national chains. They have the same reaction when newspapers sell out to distant corporate owners. In fact, the reaction may be even stronger than with other businesses because residents in communities with family owned newspapers have a strong sense of ownership: It's "my newspaper," they feel.

The newspapers in the case studies have deep family pride in their legacy as newspaper owners. Even in the face of enormous challenges to their businesses, they seemed dug-in and unwilling to sell out to a media conglomerate. They said they regularly get offers to sell. One even said his standard reply is, "Yes, the newspaper is for sale—every day for fifty cents." Resisting those offers has long been a commitment, one they learned from their parents and grandparents. Some papers have even taken steps to preserve independent ownership. Succession planning is always on their minds, and the publishers note that it's rare for a third generation to pick up a family business. In one case, the fourth generation is running the newspaper, and they are hoping a fifth generation family member will step up. All of the publishers noted an awareness of their influence in the community and were conscious of their role as newspaper owners. They all support philanthropic efforts, saying they feel a strong sense of responsibility to their communities.

One of the biggest plusses for family owned newspapers is their ability to independently control their numbers—whether it's advertising rates, the price of the newspaper, profit margins, or staff size—without consulting others.

When it comes to staff size, family newspaper owners are by far less likely to cut staff than are public companies. Staff cuts in recent years have become a preferred way to cut costs in the industry. All of the family newspaper publishers said it is hard to lay off staff because of their close-knit company culture. They said it also was harder for them to make those decisions because turnover in many positions is notably less than at public companies. Knowing staffers for years impacted their decisions about cutbacks. Consequently, their preferred staff reduction strategy was attrition and leaving some positions unfilled. The managers at the family owned newspapers appreciated the fact that they had input into staff size and were not directed by executives at headquarters to "cut twenty positions by Friday," for instance. Staff cuts were by far the most difficult decisions all the managers said they had to make. They were aware that staff cuts impacted the quality of the product and their ability to please their customers. Consequently, job security for employees and loyalty to owners can be greater at family owned newspapers.

Readers often feel a strong connection to their newspaper, especially if a local family runs it. Publishers of the locally owned newspapers said that readers don't hesitate to express their approval or disapproval of the job their newspaper is doing. Of course, readers in cities where newspapers are publicly owned are fearless about speaking up, too. But the fact that a family owns a newspaper and a publisher and his family have lived in a community for generations does seem to make a difference in reader loyalty.

The Negatives

In addition to the positive characteristics of family owned newspapers, there are some strong negatives associated with family ownership. Among them are:

- Limited resources
- Lack of strong corporate backing
- Limited support services
- Poor succession planning
- Being too close to their communities
- Family squabbles
- Lack of company diversity

These negatives, especially a lack of succession planning and family disagreements, can undermine a business and force owners to sell. But even a decision to sell for them is a local one.

Family owned newspapers can struggle with limited resources and the lack of strong backing and support from a large corporation. That being said, capital expenditures are challenging at all newspapers today. Decisions to replace equipment and make facility improvements are always contingent upon return on investment. The extent of the return and the ultimate value of the property itself, however, separate publicly owned from family owned newspapers. Family owned newspapers lack the ability to capitalize on other newspapers' successes in a large chain. While family owned companies usually make their own decisions faster than publicly owned ones and with far less red tape, they don't have the advantage of a network of properties that serves as both a testing ground for new equipment and technology and a cushion for experiments that fail to produce expected results. Knowledge of technology can be lacking at family owned newspapers because of their isolation, unless they consciously seek out other newspaper owners and operators with whom to share their experiences.

Support services are usually stronger at publicly owned newspapers than at family owned ones. But publicly owned newspapers tend to apply the one-size-fits-all strategy, especially when it comes to operating procedures. This oftentimes is cumbersome and far less effective and efficient than the streamlined operations at family owned newspapers. At family owned newspapers, though, there is no group at headquarters who can help with complex problems or offer a broader view. One solution family owned newspapers have tried is to name outside members to their board of directors, a strategy that appears to have brought some success. Another is partnering with other independent newspaper owners to obtain better pricing from vendors, for instance for newsprint. And they collaborate on studies with other independently owned newspapers so they can compare results.

Lack of succession planning and family squabbles are huge hazards to the survivability of family owned newspapers. While some families have strong legacies that date back decades, keeping a family in a business past a third generation is very difficult. Younger family members more distant from the company founders than their parents often see career paths outside the family business. Owning a newspaper, like owning a family farm, just isn't as attractive to some young people today. They aren't drawn to what has been described as a mature industry with an uncertain future, especially one forced to redefine itself in a daily struggle to survive. In addition, family disputes can result in lawsuits and ultimately force families to sell. Unless disagreements can be solved, family problems can spell death for the business.

Newspaper families can get too close to their communities, which can be bad for business, or they can suffer from their ancestors' controversial ties to community causes. Some newspaper owners in the past were less bound to the principles of editorial independence and objectivity and used their newspapers as platforms for personal agendas. Succeeding generations were then forced to try to rebuild family names and reputations, a task that can prove very difficult if readers and local advertisers harbor years of resentment and bias. Newspapers by virtue of their mission have long been both loved and hated in their communities. But the challenges of overcoming the actions and prejudices of earlier generations can add overwhelming pressure to a local publisher at a time when every decision is a critical one. Many family newspaper publishers feel a strong sense of responsibility for their community and engage in community projects to further goals they believe will enhance their communities. But family involvement can make community projects difficult for the newsroom to cover without seeming biased, and the community can react negatively if a project is seen as benefiting the family's company. These can be very difficult obstacles for the family to overcome.

Finally, some family newspaper companies own only one newspaper, and that is the sum total of their family business. But those that have made decisions to diversify and are able to invest in other businesses—real estate, television stations, paper mills, or new media ventures, for instance—are more insulated from today's tough financial environment simply because of additional revenue streams that can offset one unit's losses. While family owned newspaper publishers have always needed to be wise in business, today they must be ever smarter, savvier, and more willing to take risks. Many are expanding their businesses, offering new products, and embracing new technology. They must also be willing to learn lessons from their publicly owned peers—and many are.

A Quantitative Comparison

A study by the Independent Newspaper Group (ING) based on the Inland Press Cost and Revenue Study and prepared by John Mennenga in spring 2006 shows results at independent newspapers mirror industry trends. The study's conclusions were based on numbers for both ING member newspapers and a group of peer newspapers closest to the ING papers in circulation and either owned by a group or private. The study found that:

- "Most ING papers continued to lag public peers in all financial results measures.
- "The gap for non-core measures is less than for core products.
- "Most revenue measures match peers.
- "Most expense measures lag peers.
- "Production, salaries, and benefits are the biggest laggers."

As for trends at the ING newspapers, the study concluded that:

- "Core product margins are falling.
- "Non-core product margins are improving.
- "Total operational margins are falling as non-core product revenues represent only 10% of total operations.
- "Non-core product revenues are increasing dramatically faster than core product revenues.
- "Advertising revenue increases are inflationary, and circulation revenues are declining.
- "Benefits expense is increasing faster than other expenses."[1]

In an interview in mid-2007, Mennenga said he supported the theory that family owned newspapers may be better positioned to weather the challenges newspapers face in the twenty-first century "if they can avoid family pressures." He said family owned newspapers simply don't need the same levels of profitability that the chains do to satisfy shareholders. In many cases, they don't need the same growth of revenues that chains have to maintain. Additionally, there is more community connectedness and community support at family owned newspapers. Making their cities a better place to live "drives a lot of families, and it doesn't drive the groups," he said. That's not to say that the chain newspapers don't support community activities. They certainly do, Mennenga said. But a family can contribute millions of dollars to build a state-of-the-art music center, for instance; whereas, a public company would not. It's simply a different point of view.

For years, Mennenga has facilitated financial benchmarking for members of Independent Newspaper Group, which consisted of thirty-two newspapers for fiscal year 2005. ING newspapers are defined as "non-public, non-huge," private[2] papers. The *Washington Post*, which is family controlled but publicly traded, for instance, would not qualify for membership. ING members are individual newspaper companies that may own two, three, or four smaller newspapers but don't have the same synergies as the large groups in the country. Some nonprofit foundations can be included, and there are papers of all sizes. The 2005 study included newspapers with weekday circulations ranging from 28,000 to 334,000 and Sunday circulation from 34,000 to 457,000. ING newspapers were broken into categories by circulation size and compared to peer-size group newspapers.

The study showed ING papers were lagging public papers in all financial measures. Mennenga said that has been a long-term trend for a variety of reasons. "They [ING papers] do have different values, and they are willing to sacrifice margins and cash flow for reasons of community involvement, employee improvement, etc. Another reason is they sometimes simply don't have the efficiencies of the critical mass and scale that the big publics do." ING papers can't get the same terms from many of their suppliers, for instance. But there are agencies like PAGE, a co-op that helps them buy newsprint at costs reasonably close to what the chains pay.

The study shows that core-product margins are lower at ING papers than at groups—11 percent for ING papers versus 13.3 percent at groups. The same is true of noncore product margins—26.7 percent for ING papers versus 28.1 percent for groups. "That's partly scale as applied to the family papers, partly concern for employees, etc.," said Mennenga. But that doesn't mean the ING papers are less efficient in production. "Part of the difference has to do with accounting principles, and one really has to take that into account for all of these measures, that some papers will load their noncore expenses into their core product and others will not—they will fully allocate. So the consistency among the chains is greater than it is among the families because the chains typically can mandate how things will be accounted for so they can achieve the reporting consistency that is lacking among ING papers."[3]

So, are ING papers doing more noncore product development than the group papers? Not necessarily, Mennenga said. Some are very aggressive and innovative, like the *Bakersfield Californian*. Some papers try many things, fail at some but keep trying. At others, noncore, which includes commercial printing revenues, is very high. Mennenga cited the *Gazette* in Cedar Rapids as doing millions of dollars of commercial printing because they invested in a new printing plant that could print comics and other commercial printing projects. The *Fayetteville Observer* does commercial printing for customers in the Southeast, which brings in millions of dollars a year. Other papers "have no noncore product revenues except electronic. They don't own any weeklies; they don't have any niche publications; they don't have any commercial printing," said Mennenga. At these newspapers, there is very little nontraditional revenue, he said.

Total operating margins and total cash flow are lower at ING papers than at group papers. The numbers show total operating margins of 12.5 percent at ING papers versus 15.9 percent at group papers. Total cash flow is 18.0 percent at ING papers compared to 20.6 percent at group papers.[4] The reason is simple: ING papers have lower margins, so cash flow is understandably lower for the same reasons mentioned above.

Core product revenues per copy were $605 for ING papers compared to $587 at group papers. Per copy is the result of operational data, such as revenues or expenses, divided by daily circulation. Noncore product revenues per copy were $65 at ING papers and $64 at group papers. Total operations revenues per copy were $675 at ING papers and $650 at groups.[5] That might mean less aggressiveness to sell at group papers. But, Mennenga points out, when group newspapers reduce staff, they typically do not reduce revenue-producing staff. He cited an example of a publisher announcing about thirty-five full-time equivalent (FTE) reductions and pointing out that they would not come from advertising or circulation sales efforts but rather other departments, including editorial, maintenance, etc. "FTEs in advertising are typically somewhat lower in the family papers than in the groups," he said. "I think the family papers are more equitable when it comes to cuts in FTEs." One newspaper he cited did the opposite of what groups do when it came to staff cuts. They maintained editorial while reducing circulation and advertising sales, which likely contributed to their revenues and their noncore product revenues lagging other papers. "The more people you have selling, the more likely you are to sell something."

The groups have one big advantage over ING papers in that they have corporate headquarters that will work for them with national advertisers. Mennenga said he thinks family newspapers fall under the radar screen of Newspaper Services of America and Print Media Inc., companies that place hundreds of millions of dollars a year of business advertising into newspapers through inserts. "They are much more likely to deal with Gannett corporate or Lee corporate to be more aggressive in negotiating prices" than they are with an individual ING newspaper, which is hardly noticed.

The benchmark study showed revenue streams of core versus noncore products were about even for ING and the group papers—90 percent for ING papers compared to 91 percent for group papers. The reasons are simple. "Everybody is really pushing the web. Everybody is really trying to push niche publications, weekly products, anything they can do," Mennenga said. He said he thinks the group papers could be more experimental. In the past, "for Scripps, Evansville, Indiana, was kind of a beta site. They would test things there and if successful roll them out to the other papers. If they were not successful, they would either curtail the project or they would try it at another paper in another fashion. Of course, families can't be quite that experimental. They have to make things successful. They can't bet the ranch." He said in some instances, however, "families are more flexible in that they don't have to go though a corporate hierarchy to get permission to do things. They make the decision instantaneously; whereas, a Gannett paper has to go through regional to corporate, and so on."

Core product expenses per copy were $540 at ING papers versus $502 at group newspapers, according to the study. Noncore products expenses per copy were also higher at ING papers, $50 at ING papers compared to $42 at group papers. Total operations expenses per copy were $590 at ING papers compared to $555 at group papers. Mennenga said typically ING papers have more staff. ING papers have higher costs and higher expenses than do the groups. "Whether that's efficiency or whether that is family values, what are the tradeoffs there—to the extent that family papers are less likely to have immediate FTE reductions and so on, as the groups are when they've failed to meet analysts' expectations."

Advertising revenues per copy are higher at ING papers, at $480, than at group papers, at $472. Circulation revenues per copy were also higher—$121 at ING papers versus $109 at group papers. ING papers have the ability to independently set rates, but not necessarily more than groups do. "Both have the same competitive environments," Mennenga said. "The old days of newspapers being a noncompetitive medium are obviously no longer true. There's more than enough competition out there to go around now." He said Warren Buffett used to say newspapers are like an unregulated public utility, but he doesn't say that anymore. Mennenga said he thinks there is a reluctance at family owned newspapers to arbitrarily reduce circulation that they perceive as costing too much to maintain. He cited an example where a large chain bought a Midwest newspaper and began to shrink the area to a few counties for home delivery. They continued to have some single-copy sales around the state, but they were not aggressively pursuing that circulation because they couldn't get advertisers willing to pay for it. "I think families are still driven a little bit more by ego, if you will. That's why they offered it." In addition, the family felt that everyone in the state who wanted their newspaper should have access to it. The chain simply didn't feel that way.

Production expenses per copy were $60 at ING papers versus $51 at group papers. It's the higher cost of materials. But newsprint and ink expenses per page were lower at ING papers at $222 than at group papers at $228. Mennenga explained that that is where the co-op PAGE comes into play. Also, Cox Newspapers offers a buying service for families. "But the other larger variable [is] the chains can buy at greater discounts, and so their costs may be less. ... But what they might do is charge the papers for newsprint, but when the newsprint prices go down, that charge does not go down. They just take the additional revenues to headquarters, which would suggest that perhaps their costs are overstated. And, in fact, they may have even lower expenses than ING papers do." In one case, 10 percent per pound of newsprint costs went to corporate, he said.

Salary expenses per copy were higher at ING papers at $225 than at group papers at $214, which would suggest that families have to pay higher salaries because they don't offer the ownership opportunities that the groups do. "In other words, the groups can offer stock options and qualified stock purchase plans," he said. But ING papers typically don't do that. There are a handful that will have what's called "shadow stock" to give the employees an opportunity to invest in the future of the company without actually owning part of it. One of the reasons is to keep people because there's no advancement ladder at the family papers like there is at the groups. If a person works at a large chain, he or she can go from a small market to a larger market, then on to a metro market. "Families typically can't offer that. They've got one paper. So you've got to pay to keep people you want. You might have to pay more than a group does."

While he hasn't surveyed the ING group recently on employee longevity, Mennenga said there have been surveys in the past that show that longevity by managers at family papers is far longer than at group papers. "About two or three years ago we did the ad directors, and the average ad director in the [ING] group had been with the paper something like twenty to twenty-five years. That is typically not true in a group environment."

Looking at benefits expenses per copy, which were $47 at ING papers and $41 at group papers, it could be concluded that benefits at family papers are better. "Some still offer both defined benefit programs and 401(k)s. That's unheard of at a public company," Mennenga said. The other reason is soaring health-care costs, which have been difficult for everyone but worse for family newspapers because they have a smaller pool of employees to spread the risks over than at a large chain. Health-care benefits tend to increase faster at the family owned newspapers, causing some of them to self-insure. The longevity also plays a role. The family papers have an older pool of employees, which drives up costs. "So, there are several reasons it's caused benefits to be more difficult for the families."

Core product margins are down at ING papers—to 11.1 percent in 2005 from 12.6 percent in 2004, an 11.9 percent change—suggesting less revenue from newspapers, which is no surprise. Noncore product margins, however, are up at ING papers—26.7 percent in 2005 from 15.9 percent in 2004, a 67.9 percent change. "You almost have to look at it paper by paper," Mennenga said. "It depends on the management style and philosophy and also the labor conditions." Some papers are not willing to experiment with noncore products for a variety of reasons, including labor union contracts. Others say that because they don't have labor unions, they have more flexibility when it comes to development. "Some newspapers are just more experimental—they just have that mindset—where others are more conservative."

Total operations margins for ING papers were down from 13.3 percent in 2004 to 12.6 percent in 2005, a 5.3 percent decrease. Total cash flow at ING papers showed a decline as well, from 18.8 percent in 2004 to 17.9 percent in 2005, a 4.8 percent decline. These numbers are no surprise given newspapers' economic trends.

But ING core product revenues from 2004 to 2005 showed a 1.8 percent increase and noncore product revenues increased 19.6 percent from 2004 to 2005. ING total operations increased 1.7 percent from 2004 to 2005. ING core product revenues declined by 3.9 percent between 2007 and 2006, while noncore revenues increased by 11.8 percent for the same period. Total operation revenues declined by 0.5 percent. Mennenga said the same trend was holding for 2008. He explained that the ING figures reflect what is also true at the group newspapers. Citing diminishing core product revenues reported by McClatchy and Gannett, he noted that all newspapers are subject to the same market forces. "The big box stores are in all markets. They often dictate the rates. Real estate is down across America. ... So everybody's subject to that. Everybody is subject to automotive manufacturing advertising. They all have Ford, General Motors, and Chrysler."

Mennenga expected flat or negative core product revenues in 2007, and that proved true. Electronic revenues increased by 16 percent in 2007 versus 2006. Niche publication revenues are increasing rapidly; whereas, the core classified categories of automotive, employment, and real estate are all negative, and many of the big box stores are flat or negative. He said the changes in retail are probably the most influential on newspapers today. Twenty years ago, the department store was the dominant general merchandise sales component. Today the super discounters are. The Walmarts, the Costcos, Sam's Club, and B.J.s account for half of all general merchandise sales, Mennenga said, and they don't advertise much in newspapers. Some newspapers get one insert a month from Walmart. Costco does no advertising except for new employees. "So these changes impact every newspaper in every market. Where the big box stores are and super discount stores are, the department stores keep diminishing."

The study showed ING noncore revenues were up 11 percent from 2004 to 2005. ING advertising revenues were up 3.5 percent, but ING circulation revenues were down 10.7 percent from 2004 to 2005. Mennenga attributed declining circulation revenues to "the substitution of less-than-full-price circulation for full price. Third-party copies, sponsored copies, those kinds of efforts to keep circulations artificially high generate less revenue than do the traditional, full-price, home-delivered copy sales. I think many newspapers have just resorted to many less-than-half-price offers." He said the Audit Bureau of Circulations has permitted the erosion of prices. Now some papers are saying they can't continue that strategy. With delivery costs going up—the price of gasoline and insurance both rising—while newspaper prices go down, there comes a point where a newspaper will say it just doesn't want to subsidize third-party copies any longer. Family papers are no different. They are relying more on advertising and the success of niche products and advertising marketing. "I think more papers are trying to respond to advertiser needs," he said, "and the playing field is much more level now with all the new competition newspapers have."

Total expenses at ING papers were up 2.3 percent from 2004 to 2005. Salaries and benefits were both up—salaries 1.9 percent and benefits 9.7 percent for the same period. Rising health-care costs as well as costs related to retirement are to blame.

In a separate study that analyzed household coverage, ING newspapers' weekday and Sunday declined in their home counties/newspaper designated market (NDM) from 1997 to 2005. Weekday household coverage dropped from 51 percent in 1997 to 42 percent in 2005. Sunday household coverage declined from 58 percent in 1997 to 51 percent on Sunday. The causes in part are changing reader habits and readers choosing the Internet over print as a news source. These figures don't reflect deliberate circulation reduction because the home county or NDM, defined by the newspaper as its core based on its circulation, is an area they are not likely to cut. That's the heart of the newspaper's circulation, Mennenga said. In some cases circulation has been relatively stable, "but the households are growing faster, so therefore the penetration levels are going down." That can happen in a place like the *St. Petersburg Times*, which has become the largest newspaper in Florida, something that has always been its goal in terms of circulation, Mennenga said. "That market is growing so fast that even if you don't keep up with the market, you're still going to grow circulation." You could watch your penetration levels go down, though.

Mennenga cited a study he said suggests that the migration of readers from newspapers to the Internet is somewhat overstated. "Over the course of a thirty-day period, for example, at the *Times-Tribune* in Scranton, only about a third of their Internet readers don't read the newspaper. Two-thirds of their Internet readers also read the paper. They read both." Some newspapers are saying they are losing readers to their websites, but in Wilkes-Barre, Pennsylvania, "it was more like 50 percent for each paper was reading the other paper's site. That is to say they buy the *Citizen's Voice*, but they want to see what's going on in the other paper [the *Times Leader*] without buying it, so they go to their website, and vice versa. But that's a rare competitive market," he said.

In a look at ING group versus peer group household coverage on weekdays and Sundays in their home county/NDM, ING newspapers did better than their peers. The survey showed ING papers had 42 percent weekday home county/NDM household coverage compared to 38 percent for groups. ING papers had 51 percent Sunday home county/NDM coverage compared to 45 percent for groups. That suggests they may spend more on editorial. Mennenga said family papers are just more in touch with their communities. "They have greater longevity in their newsroom and among their editorial staff. People feel more connected to the community than in the groups where they know they're going to move on in a certain number of years."

Ultimately, there is also a big difference between an owner and a corporate employee. "The corporate employees can come and go," Mennenga said. "They're there at the whim of the corporation. The family is not. They have roots in the community. Most of them want to continue to have roots in the community. Sometimes things happen in family affairs that don't result in that continuation." But, Mennenga said, the family newspaper owners he knows all want to continue indefinitely, as long as they have family members who are also interested in running the paper.

Having no one to continue the family business can be a death sentence. But having too many family members can be challenging as well. As long as all the family members agree that the goals of the paper are being met and the financial considerations are satisfactory, there are no problems. But if some members decide they should be benefiting more financially from the paper, then the paper begins to act like a public newspaper to satisfy those financial demands. Mennenga said that is what happened at Dow Jones. "The younger generation of Bancrofts were saying, 'Hey we're not getting very much from this huge asset that we have called the *Wall Street Journal*. And if we didn't own that asset but owned other assets, we would be doing much better with our finances than we are now.' As the money becomes spread over more and more members of the family, the income per family member gets reduced." The older generation was doing considerably better because of the way the trusts were set up, but some of the younger members wanted to sell.

That scenario can happen in other families, Mennenga said, but generally now "the families are more willing to buy newspapers to grow their companies or at least maintain them than are the publics." Gannett and McClatchy are good examples. Gannett is in a position of being a seller now. When McClatchy put up the papers for sale that they didn't want after the Knight Ridder acquisition, families who are independent newspapers owners bought some of them. Families may be in a better position today by growing. "They are going to be growing their revenues if they continue to do that [buy other newspapers], and even if the margins are pressured, the additional revenues will provide more income streams for their families. In that respect they may be better positioned than are the publics to withstand" the current environment.

If the current trends continue, Mennenga doesn't know how much longer shareholders at some public newspaper companies, Lee for example, will be patient. With the company stock off significantly in the last year and the value of the company in decline, "if I had hundreds of millions of dollars invested in that company, I would not be a very happy camper." So does a takeover by a venture capitalist become a possibility? "I think so," he said. Venture capitalists like steady cash flow, and newspapers have that. It may not be growing, but it's a very steady cash flow, much like retail companies, Mennenga said.

Important to family companies is a diversified portfolio that can help support the newspaper. He cited the *Day* in New London, Connecticut, and the owners' long-term strategy. Based on a company presentation, Mennenga concluded that the owners know the future of the traditional newspaper is at risk and if they continue to publish in the traditional fashion, they will face that risk. "So they're diversifying to the extent that they can into revenue streams, which will be diverted to the newspaper to keep it strong." They are trying to get more of their revenues into weeklies, into niche products, and other noncore product revenue streams, so they can use the profits from those to funnel back into the newspaper to support its journalistic effort going forward. "That's turning the model upside down and saying, the newspaper can't support the nontraditional; the nontraditional has to support the newspaper. ... That's a conscientious effort to keep the newspaper strong and not put it at risk." Mennenga said some critics complain about that. "But I think their chances of success are better doing that than they are in continuing to put the money into their traditional product, which is at risk. To me, that's very insightful and was done with a lot of foresight." The publisher, Gary Farrugia, is not driven like a business manager but rather like a newsman. He wants his paper strong, Mennenga said, and he feels that is the best way to do it. "I think that's the strategy perhaps more will follow in the future, which would be another way to weather the storm in a way that maybe some of the groups would not."[6]

Included in the ING study were: *Press of Atlantic City*; the *Bakersfield Californian*; *Bangor Daily News*; the *Advocate* (Baton Rouge); the *Herald News* (Passaic County) *and* the *Record* (Bergen); the *Buffalo News*; Greater Philadelphia Newspapers; the *Gazette* in Cedar Rapids; the *News-Gazette* (Champaign); the *Post and Courier* (Charleston); the *Daytona Beach News-Journal*; *Telegraph Herald* (Dubuque); *Erie Times-News*; the *Register-Guard* (Eugene); the *Fayetteville Observer*; the *Forum of Fargo-Moorhead*; *Free Lance Star* (Fredericksburg, VA); *King County Journal* (Kent, WA); *Lancaster New Era* and *Intelligencer Journal*; *Union Leader* (Manchester, NH); the *Day* (New London, CT); *Pittsburgh Post-Gazette*; the *Portland Press Herald* (Portland, ME); the *Pueblo Chieftain*; *Santa Barbara News-Press*; *News-Press* (St. Joseph, MO); *St. Petersburg Times*; the *Seattle Times*; *South Bend Tribune*; the *Times-Tribune* (Scranton); the *Spokesman-Review* (Spokane); and Swift Newspapers.[7]

The bottom line is: A family owned newspaper as an investment is simply worth more to a family than to a big publicly owned company. To a family, the newspaper is the core business. To a public company, a newspaper is one property responsible for one unit of total expenditure and revenue. Decisions are more objective and directed. Family owned newspapers play by different rules. Their decisions are more subjective and shrouded in a deep culture of tradition. For family owned newspapers to survive and thrive, they must embrace industry changes and, like generations before them, turn those challenges into opportunities. They have a long history of doing that. Family newspaper owners are no strangers to hard work and ingenuity. And they know that good journalism can be good business.

Notes

1 John Mennenga, "ING Financial Benchmarking, Fiscal Year 2005, based on Inland Press Cost and Revenue Study" (PowerPoint presentation, Independent Newspaper Group, Kansas City, MO, fall 2005).

2 John Mennenga (Independent Newspaper Group), interview with the author, July 24, 2007.

3 Mennenga, interview.

4 John Mennenga, "ING Financial Benchmarking, Fiscal Year 2005."

5 Ibid.

6 Mennenga, interview.

7 John Mennenga, "ING Circulation" (info sheet on 2006 circulation of ING newspapers, Independent Newspaper Group, Kansas City, MO, fall 2005), provided by John Mennenga.

PART TWO

Arkansas Democrat-Gazette

In Little Rock, residents embrace the charm of the South and a culture of strong conservative values and honesty. It's a typical Southern city warmed by muggy summers, the lazy Arkansas River, and friendly smiles. It's also a place where Arkansans embrace all things Arkansas. Outsiders are welcomed, but insiders are cherished. So it's no surprise that the *Arkansas Democrat-Gazette*'s success is due, at least in part, to its perception as the hometown newspaper. Owner and Publisher Walter E. Hussman Jr. has spent more than thirty years nourishing that perception and reassuring the public that his family owned newspaper is run by insiders who understand local readers and their problems.

It hasn't been an easy task, though. In fact, you could say it's been a story of one man's victory against enormous odds. For that reason, the *Democrat-Gazette* is worthy of careful study. In 2003 it reached the highest city zone penetration on Sunday of all major newspapers in the United States, a position it still held in 2007. With a Sunday circulation in 2010 of 273,125,[1] it faces the same challenges all newspapers do today. But being privately owned and run by one of the most successful newspaper publishers in modern times have given it an edge. The *Democrat-Gazette* is a model of how family owned newspapers can survive and thrive against today's changing world of corporate journalism.

It all began in 1970 when Hussman, armed with a journalism degree from the University of North Carolina–Chapel Hill and an MBA from Columbia, found his niche as a business reporter at *Forbes* magazine. Working in New York seemed far more exciting than going back to Camden, Arkansas, where his father and his grandfather before him ran a handful of community newspapers in Camden, Texarkana, Hot Springs, El Dorado, and Magnolia. He knew the newspaper business well, having worked at the *Camden News* from the age of ten. What he didn't know was that he would be swept into the viciously competitive world of corporate journalism. The tables would turn, and the once-dominant, two-time Pulitzer Prize-winning *Arkansas Gazette* would sue him in a federal antitrust case. Then he would find himself in a vicious war with Gannett, the nation's largest newspaper company trying to run him out of business. His was to become a career of survival.[2]

The Little Rock newspaper wars were about competitive newspaper strategies and not unlike the battle for survival newspapers find themselves in today. In Little Rock, it was a story of mistakes, mismanagement, misjudgments and, finally, of lessons learned. And it ultimately was a story of public versus private ownership.

First, the History

The *Arkansas Gazette* dates back to 1819 and founder William E. Woodruff, who combined it with the *Arkansas Democrat* as the *Arkansas State Gazette and Democrat* during the 1850s. He changed the name to the *Arkansas State Gazette* in 1859. A new *Arkansas Democrat* began just after the Civil War, following a series of owners and name changes. Col. J. N. Smithee bought the paper in 1878 and restored the *Arkansas Democrat* name. The newspaper passed through other owners until K. August Engel took over in 1926. When he died in 1968, his nephews, Marcus George and C. S. Berry became editor and publisher, respectively. In 1974, George and Berry sold the *Democrat* to Camden News Publishing Company, owned by Walter E. Hussman and his family, for $3.7 million, and Hussman's son, Walter E. Hussman Jr., then twenty-seven, became publisher.

The Gazette Publishing Company was reorganized in 1902, and John Netherland Heiskell was appointed president and editor in chief. Heiskell's son-in-law, Hugh B. Patterson, became publisher in 1948, and in 1970 was elected president.

By the 1950s, the *Gazette*'s circulation had reached 100,000, but the newspaper's editorial position on the Little Rock desegregation crisis cost it substantially, and the number dropped to 83,000. In early 1960, circulation at the *Gazette* had edged up to 88,152, but the *Democrat* was slightly ahead with 88,890. By 1974, the *Gazette* had gained the lead with 118,702, while the *Democrat*, reflecting a national trend of declining numbers for afternoon newspapers, drifted down to 62,405—the position the Hussmans found themselves in the year they took over.[3]

Hussman said they knew it would be a daunting task, but they thought they could streamline the operation and reduce costs, make a little money, and slowly increase their market share, which was only about a quarter share of the newspaper revenue at the time.

The First War: Against Patterson

When Hussman and his father bought the *Democrat*, they decided to give it three years. If by then they had not been able to turn the financial situation around, they would cut their losses and move on. By 1977, circulation at the *Democrat* had slipped to 55,000, and costs were mounting. Needing an exit strategy, a desperate Hussman offered Patterson a lucrative joint operating agreement whereby he would get 100 percent of the profits up to what the *Gazette* had made the previous year. Of the next $600,000, the *Gazette* would get $300,000 and the *Democrat* would get $300,000 to make note payments over twenty years. After that, the *Gazette* would get 90 percent, and the *Democrat* would get 10 percent.[4] But Patterson was not interested.

Patterson's first mistake was not accepting the joint operating agreement (JOA). Failing in his attempt to forge a JOA, Hussman mounted a fiercely competitive head-to-head fight centered on the newspaper's move to morning publication. He added color to the front page every day, doubled the size of the newsroom, and increased the news hole by 80 percent. He also started offering free classified ads. The *Democrat* had always tried to be a complement to the *Gazette*. "So what if we tried to be a substitute? Could we succeed?" Hussman wondered. Investigating what other number two newspapers across the country were doing, he found that the afternoon newspaper in Dallas had started a morning edition and gained circulation. "We said, look if we are going to make a last gasp effort at this, we have to do it all," Hussman said. "If it doesn't work, we need to quit. We need to know something in ninety days, and it's going to be expensive."

It did work. By 1980, the *Democrat* had become the fastest growing newspaper in the nation. Advertising and circulation revenues went from $5 million in 1974 to $18 million in 1984. Circulation on Sunday went from 91,755 in 1974 to 143,690 in 1985, against the *Gazette*'s 141,989 in 1974 and 162,606 in 1985.[5]

In 1986, the *Gazette* sued the *Democrat* in a $133 million[6] federal antitrust case claiming the *Democrat* was trying to drive the *Gazette* out of business. A jury disagreed and found in favor of the *Democrat*, Hussman, and Camden News Publishing Company on three counts of alleged violations of federal law and three counts of alleged violations of state law.[7] "It must have been tremendously disappointing to them because as recently as 1977 they could have had the whole thing. They could have had 90 percent of the profits ... elimination of any competitive threat. They looked the other way and turned it down," Hussman said.[8]

Charles W. Pearce, who studied the newspaper war, quotes former *Gazette* editor and *Democrat-Gazette* columnist Bob Douglas as saying, "I think that was a serious mistake"[9] not accepting the JOA.

Patterson's second mistake was not responding to the *Democrat*'s fiercely competitive strategies of dramatically increasing the size of the staff and the newspaper.

Max Brantley, former city editor and assistant managing editor at the *Gazette*, said the "*Gazette* never, never, never, in the Patterson era, made the commitment to newsprint expenditure that Hussman did."[10] Hussman was determined to publish the biggest newspaper in Arkansas by having the most number of pages. "More is more. And that was the story from the beginning of the newspaper war."[11]

The *Wall Street Journal* in a March 28, 1983 article notes that the *Gazette* was resistant and ignoring the *Democrat*'s gains, quoting Patterson, then sixty-eight, as saying, "You don't take an old lady like this and simply try to change her character."[12]

Patterson's third mistake was underestimating the competition. Hussman was an unknown, Jack Meriwether, former general manager of the *Gazette*, said. "He is the most self-effacing, nicest guy you ever met." But the reality is that Hussman knows what he wants and keeps his goal in mind. "He not only is willing to pay salaries, he's willing to buy newsprint," Meriwether said. "He's willing to go after it. He knows how to spend the money, and he knows how to make it."[13]

William Bowden, in a study of the Little Rock newspaper wars, quotes Tom Kemp, a former vice president for Dillard's department stores, calling Hussman an "astute businessman—very bold, aggressive, tenacious."[14] Kemp said Hussman was forced to take action—something significant—"or he wouldn't be able to keep the *Democrat* alive ... [the *Gazette*] totally underestimated Walter and his talent and ability."[15] He said there were not only "tactical errors" by the *Gazette* but "Walter was smart enough to capitalize on it, and he just walked away with the whole market. No one thought this would ever happen, but it just fell into place."[16]

It didn't exactly just fall into place. Hussman conceived of a brilliant plan to draw in advertisers. In 1978, Hussman was having trouble getting advertisers, especially since the *Gazette* had 80.42 percent of the total ad market.[17] So he offered Dillard's, Sears, JCPenny's, and Montgomery Ward a deal where they could run their *Gazette* ads in the *Democrat* for $1 a column inch. They were paying about $7 a column inch in the *Gazette*. Bowden quotes Hussman as saying, "The *Democrat* figured at $8 [to advertise in both newspapers] vs. $7, the advertisers would realize they would be better off to duplicate their ads in both papers rather than run only in the *Gazette*."[18] The plan worked, and the advertisers agreed. "As a result, the policy did not hurt the *Gazette*, but it certainly did help the *Democrat*," Hussman said.[19]

Patterson's last and biggest mistake was filing the antitrust lawsuit. By 1984 the *Democrat* had 36.3 percent of advertising and circulation revenues in the market, up from 26.4 percent in 1974.[20] It was then that Patterson took Hussman to court. After a two-week trial in March 1986, a jury decided in favor of Hussman.[21] Peter Max, the *Gazette*'s expert economist, had testified that despite having more revenues, advertising, and circulation, the *Democrat* "had momentum."[22]

Hussman clarifies that when his family bought the *Democrat*, WEHCO Media Inc., the newspaper's parent company, had revenues of $11.3 million compared to the *Gazette*'s $14.5 million. In 1978 when the *Democrat* went head-to-head against the *Gazette* with a morning paper, WEHCO Media's revenues were $16.6 million compared to the *Gazette*'s $22.5 million. By 1984 when the *Gazette* sued, WEHCO Media's revenues—thanks to their strong growth—were $38 million compared to the *Gazette*'s $32.2 million.[23] Philip S. Anderson, the *Democrat*'s lead attorney in the antitrust case and corporate secretary of WEHCO Media Inc., said the lawsuit also "gave the *Democrat* a degree of credibility with advertisers and readers that otherwise would have taken years of competition to achieve."[24]

That sense of reality among the staff, however, was rightfully felt. Five months after the antitrust decision, Hussman learned that Patterson was selling the *Gazette* to Gannett for $51 million and a $9 million debt assumption.[25] The thirteen-year battle with Patterson was over, but the war with Gannett was about to begin.

The Second War: Against Gannett

The war with Gannett didn't last nearly as long as the one with Patterson, but it was just as—if not more—intense. Marching into town proclaiming enough resources to bury the *Democrat*, Gannett immediately started making big changes both in the *Gazette*'s appearance and content. Page one color was splashed on the "gray old lady" of journalism, stories were cut, hard news was written like features, and the once strong voice of liberals became Little Rock's version of Gannett's corporate journalism. Readers were horrified, Hussman said. "It was pretty frightening."[26]

Ernest Dumas, a former editorial writer at the *Gazette*, remembered the day Al Neuharth, former CEO of Gannett, stood before the staff and said, "We've got deep pockets. You don't have to worry. The *Gazette* is going to be here from now on."[27]

Gannett's first mistake was changing the appearance and content of the newspaper. It became bright and flashy—one day featuring University of Arkansas–Little Rock cheerleaders wearing colorful spandex tights on page one, a move that outraged readers. "This represented what the *Gazette* had become, this one picture," Dumas said.[28]

Gannett's second mistake was alienating the staff. From the first days, Gannett faltered with the *Gazette* staff. There was no love lost between Walker Lundy, the new *Gazette* editor, and them. "He thought we sucked. Just about from bottom to top. And [he] made it very clear that he felt that way. ... He pressed all of his line editors to weed people out," Brantley said.[29] Gannett brought in a transition team to create an operational plan. They assessed each department, Brantley said, all the while assuring the staff that "the *Gazette* team would stay in place, including and up to Carrick Patterson."[30] Hugh Patterson's son served as managing editor. But Patterson's days were numbered, and he didn't last.

Gannett's third mistake was bringing in outsiders. Despite saying the *Gazette* would remain a local newspaper, Gannett brought in outsiders to run it. When Neuharth arrived on the first day in a gray limousine, dressed in a sharkskin suit, he declared they were there to win the war. "Gannett comes to Little Rock," a banner read, representing the moment.[31]

Gannett's fourth mistake was losing the Dillard's account. One of the biggest blows to the *Gazette* was losing Dillard's advertising, which, according to Paul Smith, *Arkansas Democrat-Gazette* president, amounted to about $2.2 million a year.[32] William Dillard, founder of the company, pulled out of the *Gazette* in 1988 after the newspaper published a front-page story he felt was inaccurate. A short time later, he called Hussman, who had previously told him that the *Gazette* was selling advertising to other advertisers at lower rates than what they were charging Dillard's, then the largest advertiser in each newspaper. He asked Hussman to prove it, which Hussman did by showing him invoices from other advertisers. The *Democrat* ultimately came up with a plan to meet Dillard's marketing objectives by using only the *Democrat*, and Dillard's never advertised again in the *Gazette*.[33]

Smith said the Dillard's advertising switch didn't boost *Democrat* ad revenue tremendously. "They didn't spend a lot more money with us. They just stopped spending it with the *Gazette*," he said.[34]

The War Ends

In 1988, Gannett slashed the price of the *Gazette* by more than half, a move that cost the company about $7 million a year. Smith said the *Democrat* couldn't possibly match that price cut and absorb that much of a loss, so they put more salespeople on the streets, a move that cost them about $2 million a year. Smith said in the last twelve months Gannett owned the *Gazette*, the company lost $31,293,000. "Their strategy was kind of like playing poker. We'll just keep raising the ante until this guy [Hussman] can't stay in the game."[35]

So after losing about $110 million in five years, Gannett decided enough was enough. The company pulled out of Little Rock on October 18, 1991, and sold the *Gazette*'s assets to Hussman for $68 million. The next day, the *Democrat* published a combined newspaper renamed the *Arkansas Democrat-Gazette*.[36] "I think one reason we won the newspaper war here was that it was more important to us than it was to them," Hussman said. "It was kind of the fulfillment of my career ... To them it's just another market. Plus you look at the cold hard financial side of it, and it was a lot more important to us than it was to them. The profits out of a newspaper the size of Little Rock to our overall company are a huge percent of our profits. The profits of Little Rock to Gannett would have been a very small fraction of their overall profits."[37]

Lessons Learned

So were the results of the Little Rock newspaper wars due to mistakes by Patterson and Gannett or the smart strategy of Hussman? The answer is both. Patterson missed an opportunity at a lucrative JOA and then failed to respond to innovative, go-for-broke strategies by the *Democrat*. He vastly underestimated his competitor, both in terms of acumen and resources. He was reactive, not proactive, and when he finally reacted with a lawsuit, he not only lost in court but he lost his psychological edge—both in the family and among the staff.

Gannett made some of the same mistakes, chiefly underestimating the competition and assuming an arrogant posture that they couldn't possibly lose the war. They changed the appearance and content of the newspaper swiftly and dramatically without sensitivity to their audience. From the start, they alienated the staff—their most crucial link to Arkansas readers. They brought in outsiders, who were viewed both inside the newspaper and outside in the community as having the values of a giant media conglomerate and being out of touch with Arkansas culture and politics. Finally, they lost their biggest advertiser, which may have been their fatal blow. Given the mindset of the *Gazette* players and the shrewdness of the *Democrat* management, there was only one logical conclusion.

"As we look back on this, we look back with a lot more confidence," Smith said. "We were pretty scared. We knew the financial power Gannett had ... I don't think it was that we were a lot smarter, but we had a plan and we stuck with it and we were focused. ... They were focused, but they were focused on the wrong objective. They were focused on two things—eliminating us from the market and then making a lot of money. We were focused on surviving. ... Our definition of victory was surviving."[38]

Hussman said at a Fort Lauderdale meeting of the Inland Daily Press Association in 1992 that Gannett's deep price cut may have been the turning point in the war. "To many Arkansans, cutting the price of the *Gazette* confirmed that their paper was not as good as it once was," he said. "The ... lesson we learned might be categorized as 'cutting your price may be cutting your throat,' " he says.[39] The *Democrat* won because of a long-term strategy. "We clearly understood we could not overwhelm, or rout, Gannett. They simply had too much money and firepower. But we realized we did have a chance at survival, and, that if we did survive, Gannett could not win because our survival would not accommodate their profitability goals in Little Rock."[40]

The Newspaper Today

The *Democrat-Gazette* differentiates itself from most newspapers in the United States with business strategies tested in the wars against Patterson and Gannett. As the owners face a new era of uncertainty, they do so with the confidence and strength of their past. Here are the market facts:

- The *Democrat-Gazette* has the highest city zone Sunday penetration of all major newspapers in the United States.
- "The *Democrat-Gazette* has more Sunday circulation than all of the other fourteen Arkansas Sunday newspapers combined.
- "The *Democrat-Gazette* reaches 84 percent of all MSA (Metropolitan Statistical Area) adults during an average week.
- "Seventy-six percent of adults in the MSA would rely on the *Democrat-Gazette* for their employment needs.
- "Sixty-five percent of adults in the MSA would use the *Democrat-Gazette* as their advertising source to purchase a new or used vehicle.
- "The Sunday *Democrat-Gazette* reaches 73 percent of all males and 75 percent of all females in the MSA.
- "The Sunday *Democrat-Gazette* reaches 80 percent of those people who earn $75,000 or more.
- "Each week 88 percent of Pulaski County residents read the *Democrat-Gazette*."[41]
- The *Democrat-Gazette* has more Sunday circulation than newspapers in markets larger than the Little Rock Metro Market such as Austin and Memphis.[42]
- The *Democrat-Gazette* has more Sunday circulation than Birmingham, Nashville, Charlotte, and Salt Lake City, all larger markets.[43]

The *Democrat-Gazette* has reached that success through smart business strategies made easier by being a family owned newspaper. Below are some of them.

Offer Free Classified Ads

Free classifieds grew out of sheer necessity in the late 1970s. By December 1978, after three years of losing money and market share and embroiled in a head-to-head battle with Patterson who had rejected a proposed JOA, the *Democrat* started a free classified ad program. Smith and others had heard that a newspaper in Winnipeg, Canada, had done it, so they went for a visit. Smith said the *Democrat* was the first newspaper in the United States to try it. Today, they have a formula to limit free classifieds to a manageable size of four pages. They developed a system to determine how many ads to run in each category, and when readers call asking to place a free ad, they are told when the next slot is available. If that slot is a couple of days away, they are told that they can pay to get their ad in sooner. "Probably a third of the people pay to get it in sooner," Smith said. "But even if they pay for it, it's not expensive— maybe twelve dollars or so—insignificant. It's a way to have the best of both worlds—sales and free want ads."[44] But it takes a passion to run a successful free classified program, Smith said. The *Gazette* tried it after Gannett took over, but it didn't work.

Porch the Paper

Around the same time the free classifieds started, the *Democrat* was trying to come up with a plan for total market coverage. They wanted to deliver sixty thousand copies of the Wednesday newspaper to nonsubscribers in their MSA. They kicked around delivering newspapers to porches but weren't sure they could do it and still get the papers delivered on time. So one morning they decided to run a test. Hussman jumped into the back of a pickup truck and started tossing papers on one route while Smith, carrying a newspaper bag, placed them on porches. Smith said that during the test, the owner of one of Little Rock's advertising agencies saw Hussman. The owner told his colleagues, "'I knew it was bad at the *Democrat*, but it's worse than I even thought. I saw Walter Hussman delivering newspapers out of the back of a pickup yesterday,' " Smith said.[45]

Smith said it was an example of how the newspaper approaches challenges—by forgetting about industry norms, being innovative, and trying new things. If an idea works, they keep it. If it doesn't, they drop it. It's that flexibility in decision making that family owned newspapers have that corporate owned papers don't. No surprise. Porching the paper caught on, and the *Democrat-Gazette* continues it today. And they are not alone. Some newspapers, especially family owned ones, recognizing the need for exceptional customer service amid declining circulation, are willing to porch the newspaper.[46] "You are dressed in your pajamas. Who wants to walk out onto the street to get your newspaper?" said Lynn Hamilton, vice president of operations.[47]

Use Prepay

Most newspapers today are desperate to grow circulation. The *Democrat* was in that position back in 1987 when they found themselves up against Gannett. Hussman decided to take a smart business approach and to sell subscriptions paid in advance. "No other newspaper in the country did that," Smith said. "People thought we were absolutely insane. They said your circulation sales will dry up."[48] But that didn't happen. In fact, circulation sales averaged more than three thousand a month, three months paid in advance. Sales people began canvassing areas where they knew subscribers were likely to pay, and orders were sold over the telephone. "Everybody that promised to pay over the phone wouldn't pay, but we collected about 70 percent," Smith said. "We still do that." It's a good business practice. "It's not a good sale if you don't get the money," Smith said.[49] Today paid-in-advance subscriptions are common across the industry.

Charge for Online Access

The industry is split on charging online subscriptions. Because many Internet users believe content should be free, some newspapers allow free access to their websites. Others require users to register, and some have decided that charging for access is the way to go. At the *Democrat-Gazette*, online readers are charged a fee of about half what print subscribers pay. "We're spending millions of dollars to gather that news. Why should we give it away for free?" Hamilton said.[50] The decision to charge was made early on. There was concern from the start about the effect a free web edition would have on the print edition. "What we certainly don't want to do is cause it to hurt our print product, and we feel like a lot of newspapers are making a mistake [by not charging] because it has hurt the print product," he said. Hamilton blames the decline in single-copy sales across the country in part to free websites. "If somebody can read an obit for free on the web, why would they go buy a newspaper?" He said it is also an issue of fairness. "It wasn't fair for a subscriber in Russellville to pay for the newspaper to be delivered there, and the next-door neighbor to read it [online] and not pay anything," he said.[51]

Just Run More News

Smith said the *Democrat-Gazette* runs about 30 percent more news than typical newspapers its size.[52] When Hussman faced extreme competition in the past, he ratcheted up the game by doubling the size of the newsroom and increasing news hole by 80 percent. The newsroom hasn't suffered much over the years even during tough economic times. Staff reductions have been few, and space has been cut only slightly, Hamilton said. "I think we went from an eight-page Perspective section on Sunday down to a six. That was not really hard news. There may have been some features that we cut, but I don't think we cut actual news space," he said.[53]

Hussman received a call one day from Neuharth: "He was in an RV and he said, 'I'm not too far outside of Little Rock.' I thought he was going to stop by and say hello.' He said, 'I want you to know we had breakfast in Fort Smith with my grandchildren, and I picked up a copy of your newspaper, and I've been reading it for two hours, and I'm not finished yet.' He said, 'This is a good newspaper; there's a lot of news here.' "[54]

The newspaper takes pride in being a statewide newspaper. "We could make a lot more money if we'd cut back to about a thirty-county area, because it's expensive to truck those papers down to Lake Village or up to Jonesboro," Smith said. "Of course your penetration isn't nearly as good as it is here, so you have to subsidize carriers to deliver those papers and you lose money on it. So if we were only interested in making the most money, we wouldn't do that. There would be people in a lot of counties in Arkansas that wouldn't have access to but one newspaper, and that's the paper in the little town where they live."[55]

Operate Efficiently

The *Democrat-Gazette* has about 1,323 full- and part-time employees[56] who ultimately report to the publisher. There are fewer management layers than at corporate-owned newspapers, and staff is carefully allocated. Six people work in Personnel/Human Resources, and paperwork is kept to a minimum including written performance evaluations, which, Hamilton said, he considered a waste of time. "We don't have a lot of red tape and a lot of meaningless work requirements," he said. "At most places our size you'll see [an employee handbook] of thirty to forty pages. Our book is six."[57]

Like other newspapers, there are incentives and bonuses offered to employees who reach specific goals. In the pressroom, the lead employees get bonuses for cutting down on waste and getting the paper out on time. In prepress, workers are rewarded with free lunch for every week they go without making an error on an ad. That usually means a free lunch about three times a month. "If we can quantify something we do it, and we tie a bonus to it," Hamilton said.[58]

As for MBOs, or management by objectives, common today at many corporations, the *Democrat-Gazette* doesn't use them. Geneva Overholser explains how they work in *Leaving Readers Behind*: "By setting goals and attaching rewards to their achievement, a company can get the most out of its managers and coordinate their efforts at the same time." A survey of editors found that 71 percent said their companies use MBOs, and a majority said "that more than half their bonus is tied to their paper's financial performance."[59] The *Democrat-Gazette* also doesn't limit pay-based incentives to managers, as Hamilton notes above. Salaries are based on industry averages, and turnover is low.[60]

Hussman calls himself a "low-cost operator." He sends managers to trade shows to look for the best products, not the most expensive ones.[61] The management team makes decisions on how money is spent. When a new insert machine was needed, the decision to spend two million dollars was made even during an economic downturn. "We did that because it was time to do it because preprint volume was increasing," Hamilton said. "Because we don't have public stockholders to please and the price [of stock] to worry about, we're able to make decisions based on what needs to be done right now." There are no distant corporate executives to persuade or other cost centers to compete with.

The newspaper wars taught the *Democrat-Gazette* to be flexible and to turn on a dime. "When we saw something that wasn't working, we dropped it and went to something else," Hamilton said. "We were here in town. We didn't have to call New York to make a decision. Because our budget said one thing, that didn't mean we had to stick with it for a year. We do a budget, but if in January we realize we need to spend more money than we projected, then we spend it. It's not a problem to get approval from Walter. We learned to do that a long time ago, and we still do that today."[62]

Get Your Priorities Correct

Hussman's father taught him that the newspaper always comes first. The interests of the newspaper are more important than any of the family's personal interests. "If you take care of the newspaper and put its interest first, then all of the shareholders' interests will be taken care of."[63] For Hussman, it's readers first, advertisers second, employees third, and stockholders last.[64] Hussman said privately owned newspapers can focus more on long-term results than short-term ones, which is perhaps their greatest advantage. It is a luxury to not have to report quarterly results to Wall Street. "If you are locally owned, that's great because someone local who lives there will take a real interest in the community and try to improve the community," he said. People in the community can pick up the phone and call the publisher and say, "I want to come see you about something." You can sit down and talk to them. "You're neighbors, and you have the same community interest."[65]

The *Democrat-Gazette* and other family owned newspapers are different from how David Laventhol, former publisher of the *Los Angeles Times* and *Newsday*, describes daily papers today. They are "less distinctive institutions, less connected to their communities, more homogenized, often led by people whose only instinct seemed to be to increase shareholder wealth."[66] Tim Hay, who owned the *Press-Enterprise* in Riverside, California until 1997, says he "still holds to the belief that independence is more than a nice sounding label. It's often the key to quality and prestige taking priority over this year's earnings ... and to a newspaper with strong journalistic values and a bond with its community. ... A newspaper ought to be owned by the people in the community it serves."[67]

Publicly owned newspapers often reward successful managers by moving them to larger markets, a situation that creates revolving-door leadership and short-term thinking. Smith said the goal at a big corporate-owned newspaper is always to move up and on, and that keeps managers from having long-term strategies. "You do something that's expensive today, and you don't get a return on it for three years," he said. "That's liable to cost you your job or at least your promotion. Why invest in something that is going to benefit the guy that replaces you?"[68]

Most of the management team at the *Democrat-Gazette* has been there for at least twenty-five years and some more than thirty, including President Paul Smith, Vice President of Operations Lynn Hamilton, Advertising Director John Mobbs, Circulation Director Larry Graham, and Treasurer Allen W. Berry. Despite offers over the years, they plan to retire from the *Democrat-Gazette*.[69] Weathering tough times and celebrating the good ones have cemented the management team's bonds.

The Final Word

Roy Reed, former journalism professor at the University of Arkansas and former reporter at the *Arkansas Gazette*, believes "the quality of a newspaper depends, more than anything else, on its owners."[70] Hussman's ability to create loyalty is key to his success, Anderson said. Hussman was intensely loyal to his father, Anderson said, and his staff is intensely loyal to him. "But you don't have loyalty unless it's a two-way street."[71]

Smith said Hussman is different from most newspaper publishers. "He is not focused on earning as much money as he can," Smith said. "He wants a good return on his investment, but he's not willing to sacrifice quality in his newspapers to maximize profit. Walter takes pride in publishing a very good newspaper." He's a man who is committed, highly focused, low key, and easily underestimated by those who don't know him.[72]

Hussman has proven that he is a master at turning the most daunting challenges into historic successes. Family newspaper ownership gave Hussman an edge, but smart business strategies took him to victories. As newspapers navigate the turbulence of a twenty-first century media environment, they can look to the *Democrat-Gazette* as a model for survival and success.

In February 2009 the *Democrat-Gazette* reduced its workforce of about 1,300 employees by about 4.5 percent. The company had asked employees in January to volunteer to work fewer hours. In 2008, the company instituted hiring and wage freezes. Citing continued advertising revenue declines, Smith says, "It's not so much ... a desire to make a lot of money, but it's just a desire to not get ourselves into such a hole ... that we can't come out of it. Nobody knows how much longer this is going to last and how much worse it's going to get."[73]

Notes

1 *Arkansas Democrat-Gazette* Advertising, "Reach and Circulation," http://showtime. arkansasonline.com/adv/index.php?page=reach (Sept. 8, 2010).
2 Walter E. Hussman Jr. (owner/publisher, *Arkansas Democrat-Gazette*), interview with the author, Nov. 8, 2003.
3 *Arkansas Democrat-Gazette*, "Arkansas's past entwined with newspaper's vivid story," History of the Arkansas Democrat-Gazette, *Arkansas Democrat-Gazette*, http://www. arkansasonline.com/tools/newspaperhistorymain.
4 Hussman, interview.
5 *Arkansas Gazette Company v. Camden News Publishing Company*, No. LR C 84 1020 (E.D. Ark. 1986), Defendant's Trial Exhibit # 548, and Hussman interview.
6 Mark Fitzgerald, "A veil of secrecy: Rumors suggest end to Little Rock newspaper war," *Editor & Publisher* (Oct. 5, 1991): 35.
7 Walter E. Hussman Jr. (owner/publisher, *Arkansas Democrat-Gazette*), e-mail message to author, Aug. 3, 2004.
8 Hussman, interview.
9 Charles W. Pearce, "They Both Bled Red, The Little Rock Newspaper War" (master's thesis, University of Arkansas, 2000).
10 Max Brantley, interview by Ernest Dumas, Feb. 25, 2000, Arkansas Gazette Project, Pryor Center for Arkansas Oral and Visual History, Special Collections, University of Arkansas Libraries, Fayetteville.
   URL: http://libinfo.uark.edu/SpecialCollections/ACOVH/default.asp (accessed July 27, 2004).
11 Ibid.
12 Neil Maxwell, "Newspapers Slug It Out in Little Rock, Ark., And Some Say That the Readers Are Losing," *Wall Street Journal*, March 28, 1983.
13 Jack Meriwether, interview by Ernest Dumas and Roy Reed, Nov. 28, 2000, Arkansas Gazette Project, Pryor Center for Arkansas Oral and Visual History, Special Collections, University of Arkansas Libraries, Fayetteville.
   URL: http://libinfo.uark.edu/SpecialCollections/ACOVH/default.asp (accessed July 27, 2004).
14 William Bowden, "Northwest Arkansas Newspapers at War" (master's thesis, University of Arkansas, 1998).

15 Ibid.

16 Ibid.

17 Hussman, e-mail message to author, Sept. 22, 2008.

18 Bowden, "Northwest Arkansas Newspapers at War," and Hussman.

19 Ibid.

20 *Arkansas Gazette Company v. Camden News Publishing Company*, No. LR C 84 1020 (E.D. Ark. 1986), Defendant's Trial Exhibit # 596.

21 George Wells, "Antitrust verdict favors Democrat," *Arkansas Gazette*, March 27, 1986.

22 Hussman, e-mail, Aug. 3, 2004.

23 *Arkansas Gazette Company v. Camden News Publishing Company*, No. LR C 84 1020 (E.D. Ark. 1986), Defendant's Trial Exhibit # 602.

24 Philip S. Anderson (the Democrat's lead attorney in the antitrust case and corporate secretary of WEHCO Media Inc.), interview with the author, Nov. 8, 2003.

25 Bob Stover, "Gazette sold to Gannett Co.," *Arkansas Gazette*, Oct. 31, 1986, and Hussman interview.

26 Hussman, interview.

27 Ernest Dumas, interview by Roy Reed, Oct. 24, 2000, Arkansas Gazette Project, Pryor Center for Arkansas Oral and Visual History, Special Collections, University of Arkansas Libraries, Fayetteville.
    URL: http://libinfo.uark.edu/SpecialCollections/ACOVH/default.asp (accessed July 27, 2004).

28 Dumas, interview.

29 Brantley, interview.

30 Brantley.

31 Brantley.

32 Paul Smith (president, *Arkansas Democrat-Gazette*), personal interview, Nov. 8, 2003.

33 Hussman, e-mail, Sept. 22, 2008.

34 Smith, interview.

35 Smith.

36 Hussman, interview.

37 Hussman.

38 Smith, interview.

39 Mark Fitzgerald, "The key to victory: Publisher tells how his Arkansas Democrat prevailed in the brutal Little Rock newspaper war; cites competitor's blunder," *Editor & Publisher* (March 28, 1992): 17.

40 Ibid.

41 *Arkansas Democrat-Gazette, Market Facts*, Little Rock/North Little Rock: *Arkansas Democrat-Gazette*, 19.

42 Smith, e-mail, Jan. 30, 2004.

43 Hussman, interview.

44 Smith, interview.

45 Smith.

46 Smith.

47 Lynn Hamilton (vice president of operations, *Arkansas Democrat-Gazette*), interview with the author, Oct. 28, 2003.

48 Smith, interview.

49 Smith.

50 Hamilton, interview.
51 Hamilton.
52 Smith, interview.
53 Hamilton, interview.
54 Hussman.
55 Smith, interview.
56 Lynn Hamilton (vice president of operations, *Arkansas Democrat-Gazette*) to author, memorandum, 28 Oct. 2003.
57 Hamilton, interview.
58 Hamilton.
59 Geneva Overholser, "Editor Inc.," *Leaving Readers Behind: The Age of Corporate Newspapering*, ed. Gene Roberts (Fayetteville: University of Arkansas Press, 2001), 174.
60 Hamilton, interview.
61 Hussman, interview.
62 Hamilton.
63 Hussman.
64 Hamilton.
65 Hussman.
66 Gene Roberts, ed. *Leaving Readers Behind: The Age of Corporate Newspapering* (Fayetteville: University of Arkansas Press, 2001), 15.
67 James V. Risser, "Independent Papers: An Endangered Species," *Leaving Readers Behind: The Age of Corporate Newspapering*, ed. Gene Roberts (Fayetteville: University of Arkansas Press, 2001), 394–395.
68 Smith, interview.
69 Smith.
70 Roy Reed, "Giant," *Leaving Readers Behind: The Age of Corporate Newspapering*, ed. Gene Roberts (Fayetteville: University of Arkansas Press, 2001), 303.
71 Anderson, interview.
72 Smith, interview.
73 Associated Press, "Democrat-Gazette lays off 50-60," Feb. 24, 2009.

4

The Anniston Star

On the occasion of what would have been his father's 100th birthday, H. Brandt Ayers made a family decision that in effect would touch the lives of everyone in his hometown of Anniston, Alabama. He announced that his family's newspaper, the *Anniston Star*, would forever remain an independent newspaper.

Citing a "disconnect between newspapers and urban America" and an industry that often prioritizes profits over quality, Ayers came up with a plan in 2002 to create the Ayers Institute for Community Journalism. He had passed up a cash offer of fifty million dollars for the newspaper a dozen years earlier because he recognized the real value of the *Star* to the community.[1] A nonprofit foundation was established, and in 2006 the newspaper, in partnership with the University of Alabama and the Knight Foundation, welcomed the first six students into a graduate program in community journalism. "Our goal was to be a model for newspaper preservation but also a marriage of professional newspapers and journalism education," said Chris Waddle, president of the institute.[2]

But the answer to why it was so important to Ayers that the newspaper his family has owned for more than one hundred years remains independent can be summed up simply: "Basically, you care more," said Ayers, the third generation to run the newspaper. "It's a personal relationship of loving and scolding and chiding and encouraging and hurting and being hurt but always caring, like any slightly dysfunctional family."[3]

In the spirit of keeping the ownership of the newspaper in the community, on September 29, 2002, Ayers dedicated the *Star*'s new sixteen-million-dollar facility on the site of the old Fort McClellan army base. "The primary quality of a family newspaper publisher ... is a passionate commitment to one patch of earth on this planet and the people who live there. So in a sense, this building ... is a gift to the community that I have cared deeply about," he says.[4]

The Ayers Institute for Community Journalism

The idea for the Ayers Institute began with a conversation Ayers had with his wife one day while they were driving. She suggested they donate the newspaper to the University of Alabama, from which Ayers graduated in 1959. But after wrestling with the idea, Ayers decided that "giving it to the university would be like giving it to a political party or the State of Alabama."[5] Instead, they decided to form a partnership with the university and the Knight Foundation. A foundation was set up for the Ayers Institute so over time the foundation, which is tax exempt, could accept stock from members of the family. Eventually, the shares in Consolidated Publishing would flow into that foundation, and at least half of the money that would have gone to dividends would help support a graduate program in community journalism.[6]

After the company signed an agreement, the University of Alabama got a $1.5 million grant from the Knight Foundation and $750,000 from Consolidated Publishing. Waddle was named director of the master's program. A half-dozen students were admitted the first year, and two were to be added a year up to twelve, Waddle said. They are enrolled in the university's graduate journalism program, but they work and study three hours away at the *Star*. Their tuition is paid by the partnership, and students get a stipend to live in Anniston. When they finish their degree, they receive a stipend of $1,500 for a job search, and when they find a job, they get another $1,500 to help them relocate. The grant stipulated that a website be set up and a national conference held. "We're expected to be a center of thinking for community journalism, and not just a degree institute," Waddle said.[7]

Family Ownership Versus Corporate Ownership

In a city the size of Anniston, with a population of about thirty-five thousand, the *Star* has an impressive daily circulation of about twenty-six thousand and a Sunday circulation of about twenty-seven thousand. A city penetration of 60 percent[8] means that accountability is high for the staff. Ayers said the staff is doubly careful about accuracy and fairness because of the immediate feedback they get from the community. He said most of the surveys the *Star* has done indicate the community agrees with the direction of the newspaper even if they do not always agree with its political leanings.

Ayers acknowledges that the community may not care that a local family owns the newspaper, but he said if a chain came in, that would wake them up. Occasionally he has tried to raise awareness about how important family ownership of the newspaper is. He told those gathered at the new building dedication in 2002 that they should know the difference between a family owned newspaper and a corporate owned one. "If we were bought by a big corporation," he said, "the first thing to go would be the distinctive features of this building, the skylights that make it look like teepees. ... And then about a third of the building would be lopped off. You don't need all that space because they would've fired at least half of the reporters."[9] He pointed out that the *Star* has 50 percent more reporters than other comparable size newspapers. "The next thing to go would be my brother-in-law, and then after that, me. Then you'd have a newspaper that's run by a manager whose loyalty is to a corporation instead of a community," he said. Ayers said he thinks the community would rather "have the son-of-a bitch we know instead of the son-of-a-bitch we don't know."

At one Christmas luncheon, he reminded the staff how important it is to them that the company be family owned. "If this was a normal corporation, at least twenty of you wouldn't be here. But instead, we passed out Christmas bonuses today. That's the difference," Ayers told them.[10]

The *Star*'s local history dates back to the late nineteenth century when Dr. Thomas W. Ayers bought the *Jacksonville Republican*. Dr. Ayers and Dr. J. C. LeGrande, his brother-in-law, moved the paper to Anniston in 1900, changed its name to the *Anniston Republic*, and later merged it with the *Daily Hot Blast*. Dr. Ayers became editor of the new *Anniston Hot Blast*, but when he left for mission work in China, he sold the newspaper to Milton Smith. It was sold two more times, landing in 1911 in the hands of Col. Harry Mell Ayers, Dr. Ayers' son. Col. Ayers had become city editor at the *Anniston Evening Star* in 1903. The *Hot Blast* and the *Star* merged in 1912 under Consolidated Publishing Company.

Col. Ayers served as president and publisher of the *Star* until his death in 1964. His widow, Edel Y. Ayers, was chairwoman of the board until she died in 1977. Today, H. Brandt Ayers, Col. Ayers' son, is chairman and publisher, and Phillip A. Sanguinetti, Ayers' brother-in-law, is president. In addition to the *Star*, Consolidated Publishing owns the *Daily Home*, which covers all of Talladega County and part of St. Clair County; two weeklies, the *Cleburne News* in Heflin and the *Jacksonville News* in Jacksonville; and the *Piedmont Journal-Independent*. In 1997, the *Star* moved from evening to morning publication. The newspaper today still lives by the philosophy set forth by Col. Ayers decades ago: "A newspaper must be the attorney for the most defenseless among its subscribers."[11]

The *Star* has been ranked among the thirty best newspapers in the country by the *Columbia Journalism Review*, named twice by *Time* magazine as "one of the best small newspapers in the United States," won three consecutive annual awards from the Associated Press Managing Editors for local coverage of international stories, and included in "The 10 That Do It Right" by *Editor*

& *Publisher*.[12] Ayers won the 2003 American Society of Newspaper Editors Leadership Award.[13]

Ed Fowler, vice president for operations, said the circulation-to-staff ratio at the *Star* is considerably higher than the industry norm. At any other 28,000-circulation newspaper, typically there would be about twenty-eight journalists. The *Star* has fifty-four in the newsroom.[14] But the decision to have a higher circulation-to-journalists ratio comes at a price. Ayers said, "We accept much lower profit margins. Right now we're not having an operating profit at all. We're operating at a loss, so we're paying for good journalism." But the company does not lay off employees. Instead, it uses a hiring and wage freeze, such as one that went into effect on January 1, 2005.[15]

Sanguinetti, president and co-owner, said 10 percent profit margin would be good in some tough years, but this year that may not be likely. "We're flexible," he said. But with only two majority stockholders to please—Ayers and Sanguinetti's wife and Ayers' sister, Elise—Sanguinetti and Ayers make the decisions. Having autonomy and being able to control costs at the local level means a newspaper can also control the amount of resources spent on the news operation. The *Star* management style is different from a chain newspaper because "we live here and it's a little more difficult to fire people who have worked with you for twenty years and probably go to church with you and everything else," Sanguinetti said. He acknowledges, though, that an obvious disadvantage to family ownership is the inability to call corporate bosses to get more money.[16]

Fowler sees an industry in peril because of the expectation by shareholders of public companies that newspapers produce growing profits quarter to quarter. But Fowler said, "You can't do that and do good journalism. You can't do that and do good anything." His criticism of chain newspapers is that "the people who own them look at every market as if it will expand into infinity. It won't. You either had to cut costs, raise prices, or do a continuation of those year to year."[17] When the market changes, retailers open or close, operating costs skyrocket, and populations shift, a newspaper must be able to respond with market specific strategies and priorities that focus sometimes on maintaining rather than on growing. "As bad as this year's been, next year we've got a Home Depot, a Best Buy, a Target, a Walgreens, a Goody's, a Linens 'N Things opening here. So next December I'm going to be a hell of a newspaper operator," he said.

Fowler, who worked at both privately held and publicly held newspaper chains before coming to the *Star* fourteen years ago, said the economies of the newspaper business are not complicated. "You want to cut costs? Cut down on the amount of newsprint you use or cut staff. [It's] that simple," he said. That's the corporate way. "I've been there, done that. I've laid people off not because

we weren't making money, but because we weren't making enough money. ...
I just hated doing it. People who for no fault of their own did exactly what I
asked them to do, but something happened in the economy and I either had
to lay them off or I could get fired and somebody else would do it. So I did
that and I hated it.

"We've never laid anybody off here—never," Fowler said. "And this year
if there's ever a case for cutting payroll, we've got it, along with a lot of other
people. But we're not doing it. We are freezing salaries, and we're freezing
hiring. And those are unpopular and painful and we hate to do it, but the alternative is to fire ten to twenty people."

This year the *Star* will decrease the size of the newspaper. Many newspapers have a 60:40 advertising-to-news ratio.[18] But at the *Star*, the newsroom
tells production how many columns they want each day. "And we look at the
ads, and whatever that works out to be is what we do. That's exactly the way
we do it," Fowler said.

The *Star*'s move into the new facility required a major investment at a time
when analysts and others were predicting a bleak future for newspaper companies. Fowler said for the first time in fifty years the company took on debt. "I
think this building is a very symbolic gesture for the community," he said. He
recalled a speech in which Ayers said, "We could have sold this thing for forty
million to fifty million [dollars], but we didn't and we think it's important that
it's owned by a family. So we're going to invest instead of taking the money
and run, like so many people have done. We're going to put a large part of
our own resources into this project." Fowler said he thinks that announcement
made a huge impression on the community because it showed how committed the *Star* and its ownership is to Anniston. "This part of the world is our
world," he said, "and we don't answer to New York or any of those corporate"
bosses.

During discussions about building the new facility, the owners noted the
market was small but growing. Dillard's had just announced plans to move
into Anniston, and the local mall was doubling in size. But Fowler warned,
"If you live by the market, you die by the market." Between the time the
newspaper announced the new construction and Dillard's opened, there was
a big change in Winn-Dixie's advertising strategy. The grocer has since gone
bankrupt. "They're still with us right now, but who knows how long they'll
be here," he said. "We had a couple of locally owned grocery stores that sold
to Food World, so ten thousand dollars a month goes away because they're
just adding two more addresses on the circular they're running. By the time
we opened this building, I could list the advertising losses we had, and they
equaled the increase for Dillard's. So what Dillard's did was keep us level." He
said Anniston is the closest place for residents to shop at a Dillard's, JCPenny,

or Sears. With the Target, Home Depot, and other big box stores, shoppers are pulled in. "So in terms of long-term viability, I think this is a good market," Fowler said. "I think the market will grow eventually up here rather than eight miles away at the interstate because there's a bypass being built. ... Once the bypass is open, there's going to be some commercial development in this part of town." He said that is one reason the company chose the former Fort Mc-Clellan site. The company owns twenty-two acres. The building and the parking lot take up ten, and there are ten more acres of woods behind it. "Whoever has this job twenty years from now, if they need to enlarge this building or enlarge the operation, we've got plenty of room to do it." In other words, if the *Star* management did not believe in the viability of the company and the future of the newspaper, they would not have made the sixteen-million-dollar investment, which included buying a new press.

Taking on debt is an important consideration for any company, but without the deep pockets of a huge parent corporation, a family owned business must be especially cautious about balancing liabilities to assets. Consolidated Publishing Company spent three million dollars for the new press three years ago. Newspapers that do a great deal of commercial printing can spend nine million dollars or more for a press. Fowler said at the time he told vendors: "If I buy a Chevrolet to get me from here to here every day, it'll do it. If I buy a Mercedes to get me from here to here every day, it'll do it. I can't afford a Mercedes. I can afford a Chevrolet, so that's what we bought." He said the company is careful about not overextending themselves. "I felt a tremendous responsibility in this building not to leverage this company to the point we couldn't do what we want to do."[19]

Community Journalism

To Ayers, community journalism, at the heart of the *Star*'s operating philosophy, is not a matter of geography but "a matter of attitude." Caring counts, he said. "I believe if you are in a town for a week and you read its newspaper and you have no idea about the culture of that place, then that newspaper is failing. If it doesn't have a connection, it doesn't really care about the place and the people who live there."[20]

Waddle believes there is a misconception that community journalism only exists at small papers. But there are examples of community journalism at large newspapers, the *Wall Street Journal*, for instance. "Theirs is a community of business and finance. That certainly is a community," he said. On 9/11, one of the best examples of community journalism was seen at the *New York Times*, which ran obituaries and photos of as many victims as they could. Waddle calls that "simply hometown journalism." The *Times* used the same type of coverage to document the struggles Manhattan went though covering decisions on the future of the disaster site. Other examples are the *Orange County Register*, a "huge newspaper that has decentralized itself so that it is less and less of a conventional newsroom and more and more a field of bureaus. And the leadership is out there on the other end of the spokes, not up there at the hub, which is just a production center."[21]

Like Ayers, Waddle said he thinks community journalism is a state of mind. "Do you decide for a community what it will read and what the issues are, what the stories will be? Do you drive the news into the mind of the community, as most metro papers by necessity do, because it's mass marketing? Or are you, in fact, as a journalist a part of that community so that the news begins to rise up from around you?"[22] He said the real question is who is generating the ideas—somebody sitting in an office, or is it a system of parroting what's on the mind of the community and reporting what is on the community's agenda?

Readers are not easily fooled, and they know if the profits of a newspaper are not staying in the community and if the editors and publishers are on a rotation, as is common at chain newspapers. Waddle said he agrees with Philip Meyer who argues in his book, *The Vanishing Newspaper*, that what is really of value at a newspaper is its integrity. "It's that relationship between readership, community, and the people who produce it," Waddle said. "But it's really hard to establish that rapport with an absentee landlord or with transient executives. So even good intentions, good stories, are clouded." They are handicapped without a local voice.

Local voice is important and connects with a community especially if readers have heard it all their lives, as they have in Anniston. "The voice of corporate journalism is tinny and has a funny accent and doesn't seem that familiar," Waddle said. Chain newspapers engage in cookie-cutter journalism. They look the same in cities across the nation, and there is no unique character that sets a newspaper apart. Corporate journalism tends to iron out the eccentricities and to sandpaper off burrs. "There's a homogenization and pasteurization about it," he said. "Pick up a homegrown newspaper, and it has lots of oddities, eccentricities."[23]

At the *Star*, some letters to the editor are highlighted by stars, which means editors thought they were exceptional letters. At the end of the year, writers whose letters got stars are invited to a banquet. "It's really a tremendous event that we've done for seventeen years," Waddle said. "How many corporate publishers worried about their bottom lines are going to buy that many steak dinners for that many people and spend that kind of money?"

Waddle said he thinks the future of journalism will be community journalism because the value of smaller newspaper is greater than ever. Ad rates and circulation are more stable than big corporate-owned newspapers. Community newspapers are in more manageable markets, and they don't have stockholder and Wall Street pressures. "We can be nimble. We can have good ideas," he said, defining community journalism by what drives a newspaper. "Is it a profit motive, which drives mass-circulation journalism? Or is it a community ethic, the community conscience, a wanting to preserve community, wanting to preserve the voice of the community?" Where newspaper executives have the right kind of motivation, he said, they will find the means to not only survive but also have a better chance of thriving. Smaller newspapers have the ability to maneuver against the market forces that are coming to bear against all newspapers.

Waddle said the story of the *Anniston Star* and other family owned newspapers point to a value that the public does not want to lose. "Ultimately, with journalism, the public decides, the community decides. If your survival is up to that guy down in Coral Gables, I'm sorry for you. If your survival depends upon people who really feel good that your paper connects them and helps them define themselves as a community, then you've got something really special. And I don't think the public is going to let you slip away."[24]

Community journalism at the *Star* is "local, local, local," said Troy Turner, former executive editor. The *Star* is known for localizing international news. The newspaper has won APME's International Perspective Award three times. An example of how the *Star* localizes an international story was its coverage of the war with Iraq. "We sent a reporter and photographer like a lot of other newspapers," Turner said. "The difference was we didn't go to cover a war. We went to cover a local story that happened to be occurring in a war." One of the city's largest employers was involved in the repair of armored vehicles, some in Anniston and some overseas where the company sent workers and set up repair camps. "And we billed it as if our lives depend on it—theirs do. That was the slogan of one man's workstation. This man is one of our readers; he's one of our workers; he's one of our family people."[25]

The *Star* looks for international stories to write locally. One story was about how Vietnam has captured the catfish market in Alabama. "Catfish—how much more Alabama can you get than catfish?" Turner asks. "So here is a story that explains, 'Hey, that catfish at your favorite country restaurant may actually be from Vietnam.' " The *Star* also tackled a story about whether women who wear scarves for religious beliefs should be allowed to wear them in their Alabama driver's license photos.[26]

Like any family owned business in a community, a family owned newspaper publisher can have close ties to the community. Bob Davis, editor at the *Star*, acknowledges that Ayers and other family members are highly connected to the community because of their deep family roots. But he does not seek advice on editorials or send columns to the publisher for prereview. Editorial writers wrestle with opinions but are free to take an independent voice. "Brandy doesn't see what we do until the paper comes out," he said. One priority for the *Star* is education reform, an issue that also is a priority for Ayers. Davis said he does not think editorializing for education reform is self-serving, but rather community-serving. "That the publisher, the owner, has taken an active role in this—we would've made this a priority regardless. I think anyone would come here and find that's a priority."[27]

The *Star* has an ombudsman, a journalism professor who works as a freelancer and serves as a media critic in a monthly column that focuses on the newspaper. Davis said the newspaper runs every letter to the editor that is not libelous and that stays within their rules of length and fairness. "We run letters to the editor that I'm sure wouldn't get printed in a large paper like I used to work for, and I kind of like it," he said. Giving readers the chance to respond to what they see in the newspaper is part of greater access to community journalists. "If you've got something you really want to let us have it [about], I love saying, 'Great, we'll get it right in the paper. Clean it up, put it right in," Davis said.

When irate readers call to complain, the first thing Davis does is thank them for reading the newspaper and being so moved by something that was written that they bothered to call. "We want to hear people, hear what they have to say," so he respectfully listens to them. "And we're going to offer them an input to put that in the paper. It doesn't just apply to family owned newspapers, but how many giant retailers would put a letter of complaint that they received in a prominent spot somewhere in the store?"[28]

Growth Areas

Times haven't always been flush for Anniston and its residents, but Ayers is optimistic about the future—both for the community and the company. For decades Anniston was a heavy metal town with manufacturing jobs that paid well. But plants closed, PCBs were found in the soil, and residents got sick. Fort McClellan closed. There were spikes and valleys, but through it all the *Star*, over a fifty-year period, maintained a steady increase in profits, sales, and circulation. By the 1960s, "our figures were going up, even through there was a general decline," Ayers said. "We now mirror the national economy more closely. We're not showing a continual uptake because of all of that economic restructuring of this community and all of the collateral damage from those industries; that's now all behind us."[29]

Anniston is beginning to see economic improvement because of its location in a growth plane between Birmingham and Atlanta. "So we think that the print product five years from now will be better, bulkier, more news pages, more advertising pages. And we expect that with the hookup with the university, we'll also be one of the centers for statewide Internet broadcasting setup. The old dog will be learning a lot of new tricks. Not this old dog, but some of the young dogs around," Ayers said. He hopes Anniston will one day become a research park in a research triangle because it is halfway between clusters of research universities in Birmingham and Atlanta. With defense and Homeland Security operations already present along with the infrastructure, the community is poised to grow.[30]

Niche Publications

Newspapers often fail to see magazines as their competition, but tapping into the local lifestyle magazine market can be a potential gold mine for the company and advertisers. Newspapers across the nation, including those owned by chains, are now publishing slick lifestyle magazines aimed at upscale readers, the select market for advertisers. Fowler questions the quality of the content in many of them but said the *Star* aims to do a better job with the one they developed called *LongLeaf*. "We've got a good plan put together, got a good team of people working on it," he said.[31]

LongLeaf started out with four issues in 2006, and in 2008 the staff had determined that the market the magazine serves (Calhoun, Cleburne, Etowah, and parts of Talladega and St. Clair counties) was best served with a quarterly publication. "The quarterly deadlines are critical for creating the necessary editorial content and to meet the high standards that Editor in Chief Josephine Ayers and her staff have set," said Robert Jackson, vice president of sales. *LongLeaf* advertising sales have increased year to year, which is a testament to the attractiveness of the magazine as well as an improved sales effort by the *Star*'s advertising sales team and graphic artists."[32]

Fowler said the problem with upscale lifestyle magazines is distribution. The *Star* is considering a combination of delivery by carriers and placement in bookstores. Mail distribution is also an option. Distribution will not be confined to Anniston but rather extend to northeast Alabama. "We know where the rich folk live."[33] He said the potential profit from the magazine is the driver.

In keeping with a national trend, circulation at the *Star* has shown declines. "We made a decision two years ago that we were no longer going to do churn," he said. Churn is the number of new orders the newspaper has to write to replace those subscribers who leave. "We were firing the telemarketers, we were paying enormous costs per subscription, we weren't keeping them three months, and we had to keep churning to keep up."

He concluded that the company was paying telemarketers huge amounts of money to bring in orders, two-thirds of which never generated any payment.

Noting that they had to pay carriers to deliver the orders whether they get paid for them or not, he decided to stop the process. After a transition where they saw some losses, Fowler said the paper has stabilized. "We have to write eighty orders a week to stay" even, he said. "At some point we're going to find the point where the paper stabilizes, where these are the people who want ink on a paper delivered to their houses or bought out of a rack every day. But in order to remain a viable company, we've got to find other ways to generate revenue. The real estate magazine is one, and *LongLeaf* is another. We're looking at doing some features kind of website, entertainment aimed at the eighteen to thirty-four demographic."[34]

Fowler was asked several years ago during construction of the new building why the company would spend three million dollars on a new press when the Internet was threatening newspapers. "The Internet is going to change my business, but I don't think it's going to have it. ... My pet line is, 'As long as there are grandmothers and refrigerator doors, the community newspaper is going to survive,' " he said.[35]

Sanguinetti said the newspaper is also looking for printing work, not smaller printing jobs but larger projects to maximize the efficiency of the new press.[36]

Managing the Internet

Several years ago the *Star* started charging for its website. A subscriber to the print edition gets free access, but others must pay for an online subscription. "It created a firestorm, an incredible firestorm of complaints," Fowler said. When he got a call from a woman in Los Angeles who complained that she read the *Los Angeles Times* and the *Washington Post* daily and didn't have to pay for them, he asked her why she wanted to read the *Anniston Star*. She told him she was from Anniston and wanted to keep up with people in Anniston, to read about marriages and deaths, etc. "I said, 'Well, I can't do that for you for free. I have to pay somebody to do this. It costs me money, and I've got to be able to justify it.' " She understood, he said. "All those things in a circle around the newspaper are going to help us keep that newspaper alive. It's not going to die, but it's going to change."[37]

Today the *Star* has seven hundred to eight hundred paid online subscriptions. When the online edition started, one staff member worked on it. Today, there is a New Media Division with six employees. "You can throw tons of money into stuff like that if you want to," Fowler said, but the company, like most family owned newspapers, is careful about controlling expenses.[38]

Dennis Dunn, the *Star*'s circulation director, believes the Internet is positioning the newspaper for the future. There may be a time when 25 percent of paid circulation is online circulation because younger readers are not resistant and prefer to get their news through the Internet. That's becoming more acceptable, he said. The *Star* claims online subscriptions as paid circulation because they get at least 25 percent of the home delivery price and there is an exact replica of the newspaper online. "Almost 3 percent of our circulation is online subscribers," Dunn said.[39]

Circulation Issues

From a circulation standpoint, being able to react quickly to market conditions is a huge advantage of family ownership. Having worked at a publicly owned chain for eighteen years before coming to the *Star*, Dunn said he finds family newspapers more open to investing in themselves with a quicker turnaround in the marketplace than at corporate newspapers. They are in a better position to take advantage of marketing opportunities because they are more flexible and able to make faster decisions. Having to submit a budget plan and wait months for approval sometimes led to missed opportunities and ineffective management at his previous jobs. "So I think that's the big plus to me from a circulation and marketing standpoint. We can stop and adjust on a dime," he said.[40]

Dunn sees employees taking more pride in their work at a family owned newspaper because they buy in to the company philosophy and its connections to the community. "Certainly you feel like you're making a difference when everything comes right back into this market. You're not sending money away and never knowing if you've helped this newspaper" but merely its investors. He said employees take it more personally when people are not happy with the newspaper.

The *Star* uses independent contractors to distribute the newspaper. There is a buy-sell relationship with the contractors, so the money they make is the difference between what they pay for the newspaper and what the customers pays for it. The newspaper has a rating structure that considers the difficulties inherent within every delivery route. There has been a big push over the last several years to convert subscribers to office pay. But despite that initiative, Dunn does not agree with the industry trend of converting to 100 percent office pay because a number of people, especially in his market, do not have checking accounts. Those are door collections. They are paying in cash and may not have a car, "so we try to be more flexible," something that is much easier at a family owned newspaper. "We haven't said, 'If you cannot write us a check or go down to the 7-Eleven and get a money order and then put a stamp on there and mail it in ... It doesn't matter whether you get a check once a month. That has to be sent in here by the fourth of the month, or that mean old computer is going to cut you off when your money runs out from last month. If you're late, you might have a discontinuation of your service.' We haven't gone that way."[41] He said 75 percent of their subscriptions are prepay, and customers can pay by credit card, check, bank draft, automatic renewal, or with cash at the door to the carrier. "Our system is tailored so that they can do that."

Carriers deliver the *Star* to the porch upon request. "We do offer whatever the customer wants as long as the carrier is not put in danger," but the carrier's expense must also be considered. "It's written in our contract that they have to deliver the newspaper to the customer's satisfaction, so we hold them accountable from that standpoint," Dunn said. In the last year, the company has balanced what the carriers receive in newspapers with the number of subscribers they have so the newspaper knows who all of their subscribers are. But even 100 percent office pay is not 100 percent accurate, because it is still left to where the carrier thinks the customer lives. Nevertheless, "we think this is a very accurate delivery system, and it gives our advertisers good quality service for the advertising they place with our newspaper," he said.

Twice in thirteen months, subscription prices have been increased to offset rises in fuel costs. The first increase was $0.50 a month. The second was $0.75 for a seven-day subscription. "Gas prices in this market went from about $1.50 a gallon in May of 2004 to over $3.00 a gallon in September of 2005. ... So everything being relative, that's a very minor increase," Dunn said. Quarterly territorial allowances were also instituted to help the carriers with the increased difficulties they have faced with higher fuel costs. There are special senior citizen rates, and auto-renew subscribers have been allowed to avoid price increase with their auto-renew, a strategy that has proved hugely successful. "We've added almost five hundred auto-renew customers just with that," Dunn said.

Changes in telemarketing laws have brought changes in marketing strategies aimed at bringing in new customers at the *Star*. The newspaper markets to new residents and former subscribers, but both are soft sells. If a subscriber has dropped the newspaper in the last month, the *Star* calls to try to renew the subscription. When time comes for a subscription renewal, the *Star* calls the customer. But they do not call customers who have never subscribed to the newspaper, who have lived in their house for six months or a year, or if they have not subscribed in a couple of years. "We do maintain a do-not-call list, but it's very small," he said.[42]

The *Star* has used kiosk sales in front of stores, and at one point that was about 75 percent of their sales. Dunn said it can be a successful strategy because people have their checkbooks or money in hand when they leave a store.[43] In 2008, kiosk sales were still important, but they have diversified their sales mix. "We get less kiosk sales and have replaced them with carrier orders and telemarketing orders. The difference is the carrier orders are paid or carrier collect, and the telemarketing orders are collected up front or billed. We do not start until the payment is received," Jackson said.[44]

Stores have gotten increasingly more reluctant to partner with because of the growing number of vendors who want to sell in front of doors. "It really is going to be a challenge for us this year to keep that program up and running," Dunn said. "So we are looking at trying to do some partnerships with our local Walmart Supercenters that would allow us to be out there, and that might mean a donation to a charity because they do allow charity giving."[45] In the past, some stores have allowed kiosk sales outside their stores if customers were given a gift card from the store as a premium item for subscribing.[46]

The *Star* has changed its philosophy of taking billed orders, and now sells paid-up-front orders. In 2008, 80 percent were paid up front before they are started. Jackson said they still have some telemarketing get started with promise of payments, but they are trying to eliminate that practice with the billed and "pay before starting" plan.[47]

With premium items or discounts and other incentives offered to new customers, the newspaper needs to get something that shows the customer is going to pay. Paid orders are sold when sales crews go door to door and at kiosks, but Dunn said it is very difficult to get paid orders from telemarketing. "But we've been able to take our churn down from 48 percent to 29 percent."

Dunn said churn trends show 29 percent is low. Normally a newspaper the size of the *Star* would be closer to replacing about 50 percent a month according to trends from 2002 to 2004. "It looks like as an industry we're doing better," he said. But depending on where the *Star* is categorized—a big 25,000 or a small 50,000—that is a good number for the industry. Churn for 25,000–50,000 circulation newspapers in 2002 was 52 percent and 47 percent in 2004.[48] So going to paid-in-advance orders has helped considerably. Carriers at the *Star* are all adults, so the newspaper does very little selling through carriers because they usually have other jobs.

One circulation challenge the *Star* faced was the closings of the military base in 2000. "We lost 10 percent of our population just like that in 2000. So that was a situation where nothing really came into this market to replace that," he said. He admits that Anniston is no longer the center of the retail market it used to be. A dramatic drop in retail sales hit between 1996 and 2002, and retail moved south along the interstate and to the north. Within the last eighteen months, however, retailing activity has shown signs of improving. "Now I believe this market is beginning to revive itself," Dunn said. New retailers, the revitalization of abandoned shopping centers, and retail along the interstate is boosting the climate.

The good news at the *Star* is that single-copy sales have grown—up 10 percent. When the newspaper rebalanced its home-delivery routes, they found that sometimes a carrier would have a vending machine to stock. Consequently those papers would count as home delivery. So, they moved what were really single-copy sales out of home delivery to get a more accurate count.[49] Involving carriers in sales and reducing will-pay orders allowed home delivery to grow in 2008. Home delivery was up over one hundred daily and two hundred Sunday. Single copy had suffered due to a Sunday price increase to $1.50 in November 2007 and was down 2 percent daily and 8 percent Sunday.[50]

The *Star* has also added convenience store chains that sell newspapers inside, and there is now more partnering with retailers as well as agreements to sell newspapers at special sporting events like races at the Talladega Speedway and at Jacksonville State University.

Positioning was learned by trial and error. Early on in their partnership with Walmart, newspapers were placed at each register. That was problematic because only four or five newspapers would fit there, they were constantly selling out, and children who climbed would pull them off. So the *Star* came up with the solution of putting the newspapers in vertical racks at the entrances and offering the $0.99 sale price. "That's another advantage of a locally owned smaller paper," Dunn said. "I have the packaging center where the papers are inserted and everything, so we did it though our packaging center. Most newspapers say, 'Oh, I have to do this through my carrier.' I do it through my employees."

The *Star* started out with one Walmart Supercenter and now has three. They negotiated an agreement with Walmart to sell the Sunday newspaper for $0.99 and brought in racks to hold hanging papers in poly bags. "If you go into Walmart and you walk into one of those big entrances, you're going to see one of our racks right there," said Dunn. He said his single-copy philosophy is "vertical is better" and placing newspapers in bags is clean and customer friendly. "We've gone from selling two hundred and fifty on Sunday there to four hundred on Sunday." How much of this is because of the ninety-nine-cent deal and how much of it is because of the bag? "I venture to say that probably half of it is just because it's in a bag and the location," Dunn said.

He said now that the *Star* has accurate numbers on home delivery circulation, that is the focus for the future. Acknowledging a loss in home-delivery circulation for the last two years, "we have to turn that trend around and get home delivery to grow more than anything," he said. The real problem is getting good people who can sell week after week. "And everywhere we turn, we have do-not-call and telemarketing regulations. If it's door-to-door sales, you have no solicitation ordinances. If you're trying to sample, then you've got litter ordinances. If you're trying to do kiosks, you've got stores that are saying, 'We only do charitable organizations out front.' They can shut us down at every turn, so it makes it very challenging for us. We have to keep reinventing ourselves."[51]

The Wired World

Davis said like the rest of the newspaper industry, the *Star* is working diligently to compete in a world increasingly connected electronically. In early 2007, Ayers challenged the *Star* as well as the rest of the company to become more digital. "We're no strangers to online success," Davis said. The *Star*'s website was voted top among Alabama newspapers by the state press association in 2005. "Still this is no time to relax," he said. "What's in the works is an extensive revamp of our web presence, one that will enhance our journalism as well as better connect the various communities within our communities."[52]

Among the developments since the digital challenge was issued by Ayers are:

- The naming of the newspaper's first mobile reporter. He will be equipped with "what I expect will eventually become standard gear for all reporters, namely a laptop that can wirelessly connect to the Internet from virtually anywhere he can receive a cell signal, a video/still camera, and an audio recorder. His mission is to put news with video/audio extras up for all hours of the day," Davis said.[53]

- New features, including those on motherhood issues, crime, fashion, prep sports, and a behind-the-scenes newsroom blog that flags upcoming stories, solicits reader feedback, and humanizes the newsroom staff.

- A series of podcasts, including one Davis produces daily. "I typically talk with a couple of reporters about their upcoming stories." Other podcasts are centered on sports beats, Davis said.[54]

- More video extras, including everything from how to tie a bow tie to football practice at the local college.

All this is a prelude—a "soft opening" is the marketers' phrase—to a revamped website that will combine the many resources of the company: the daily papers in Anniston and Talladega as well as the many surrounding weeklies. In short, the site, CheahaLive, will be the information source for the I-20 corridor stretching from Birmingham exburbs east to the Georgia state line.

Davis said the new site will connect readers to instant news, a digital version of the day's print editions, video and audio extras, an entertainment-oriented site dedicated to younger readers who aren't in the habit of picking up the daily paper, and offer places where readers can share their views and insights.[55]

"Despite some technical setbacks, we're close to launching our new digital face, CheahaLive," Davis said. "I think it puts into action Dennis Dunn's phrase of 'reinventing ourselves.' The new site won't change the fundamentals of how we approach community journalism. It will enhance, inform, and invigorate how we do community journalism."[56]

In November 2008, the Associated Press reported that the *Star* was cutting its workforce by 10 percent. "It was painful for our family and the board to make decisions we wouldn't have even contemplated in the past, but we cannot survive on continued losses," a statement to employees by Ayers and Sanguinetti said. "We will have to work with fewer hands and resources, but a leaner company does not mean surrendering the standard of excellence that has built our national reputation."[57]

Notes

1   H. Brandt Ayers (chairman and publisher, *Anniston Star*), interview with the author, Dec. 15, 2005.
2   Chris Waddle (president, the Ayers Institute for Community Journalism at the *Anniston Star*), interview with the author, Dec. 15, 2005.
3   Ayers, interview.
4   Liz Cox, "A big plan to stay small," *Columbia Journalism Review* (May/June 2003): 16–18.
5   Ayers, interview.
6   Waddle, interview.
7   Waddle.
8   Ed Fowler (vice president of operations, *Anniston Star*), interview with the author, Dec. 15, 2005.
9   Ayers, interview.
10 Ayers.
11 *Anniston Star*, "About Us," http://www.annisonstar.com/.
12 John S. and James L. Knight Foundation, "UA Community Journalism Program Will Blend Newsroom With Classroom," John S. and James L. Knight Foundation (Sept. 22, 2004), http://www.knightfdn.org/news/press_room/knight_press_releases/detail.dot?id=135941.
13 American Society of Newspaper Editors, "ASNE recognizes Alabama publisher for leadership," American Society of Newspaper Editors (April 9, 2003), http://204.8.120.192/index.cfm?ID=4493.
14 Fowler, interview.
15 Ayers, interview.
16 Phillip A. Sanguinetti (president, *Anniston Star*), interview with the author, Dec. 15, 2005.
17 Fowler, interview.
18 Fowler.
19 Fowler.
20 Ayers, interview.
21 Waddle, interview.
22 Waddle.
23 Waddle.
24 Waddle.

25 Troy Turner (former executive editor, the *Anniston Star*), interview with the author, Dec. 15, 2005.

26 Turner, interview.

27 Bob Davis (editor, *Anniston Star*), interview with the author, Dec. 15, 2005.

28 Davis, interview.

29 Ayers, interview.

30 Ayers.

31 Fowler, interview.

32 Robert Jackson II (vice president of sales, *Anniston Star*), e-mail to author, Oct. 2, 2008.

33 Fowler, interview.

34 Fowler.

35 Fowler.

36 Sanguinetti, interview.

37 Fowler, interview.

38 Fowler.

39 Dennis Dunn (circulation director, *Anniston Star*), interview with the author, Dec. 15, 2005.

40 Dunn, interview.

41 Dunn.

42 Dunn.

43 Dunn.

44 Jackson, e-mail to author, Oct. 2, 2008.

45 Dunn, interview.

46 Dunn.

47 Jackson, e-mail, Oct. 2, 2008.

48 Dunn, interview.

49 Dunn.

50 Jackson, e-mail, Oct. 2, 2008.

51 Dunn, interview.

52 Davis, e-mail to author, Aug. 23, 2007.

53 Ibid.

54 Ibid.

55 Ibid.

56 Ibid.

57 Associated Press, "Anniston Star to trim workforce 10 percent," Nov. 20, 2008.

The Spokesman-Review

Every day when publisher Stacey Cowles walks into the Red Tower that marks the *Spokesman-Review* headquarters at Riverside and Monroe in Spokane, he carries with him more than 115 years of tradition and a family legacy that has weathered a changing world. Like the three generations of Cowles who preceded him, he relies on inherently strong business acumen to succeed, especially during troubling times for newspapers. "What my dad used to say is, 'We make money to publish a newspaper and not the other way around,' " Cowles said. That doesn't mean he doesn't worry about the bottom line. "We desperately need to make money if we're going to stay in business."[1]

But how the Cowles company makes money reveals much about the *Spokesman-Review*'s survivability in the industry's uncertain future. Like most successful corporations—although unlike many family owned businesses—the Cowles know well the value of diversification. The newspaper, though the company's core business, is one unit along with a business biweekly, shopper, and other demand-distribution publications, forestland, a newsprint mill, three television stations, an insurance agency, strong real estate holdings, and a development company. Business Manager Robert Davis, who has been with the company for thirty years, said he is optimistic about the company's future because the family has been smart in their business practices. There is a bright future for this company, Davis said. "It's not going to be as bright as it once was, but the flame's not going out. ... They own other companies, and because of that, as a corporate whole, I think they have a very strong future, stronger than the newspaper by itself."

Davis said the Cowles have looked at what it takes to remain a family owned business, including the issues family businesses face that sometimes force them to sell. All of the Cowles' businesses ebb and flow, but their different business cycles allow one unit to help another that may be struggling. "That gives the *Spokesman-Review* some capital potentially to help get through some tough spots while we're sorting ourselves out like everybody else in the industry," Davis said. Those holdings beyond the newspaper provide a solid foundation moving forward. "The general press on newspapers puts a drag on everybody in general," he said, "because there's no perspective. Operating margins approaching 20 percent—that's pretty darn good. We could erode a little bit and still be a real financially healthy company."[2]

If you ask Cowles, he says he's not worried about survival but rather if the newspaper is a financially attractive investment. He said that given the margins newspapers have and the flexibility in terms of why people buy newspapers, there is room to produce smaller newspapers or less frequent ones. "There are many business models out there, and we are going to have to adapt to the new landscape," he said. That may mean free papers or targeted publications. "The core product is facing a lot of pressure right now." So why his optimistic outlook? "Maybe that's because I'm in other businesses, too, so it [the newspaper] won't be my entire livelihood," he said. Owning Inland Empire Paper Company, for example, has helped give the business a little cushion. "If we have a really awful year at the newspaper, it's easier if we've had good years in other companies. But ultimately the newspaper has to stand on its own and produce a return." He said family owned newspapers have a profit margin in the 18–20 percent range, compared to the 24–25 percent range for publicly owned ones.

Cowles, who became publisher in 1992 when his father, William Cowles III died of a heart attack, said he is not looking to buy other newspapers "unless they were right next door," and he's not looking to sell the one he owns either. "I think we probably could sell, but that is not something that's very high on our radar screen given our history." Cowles said ownership of the company is held in trust, "so we don't have to face the tax man every time a generation passes on. Our kids will have to face that." Many of the financial pressures have been eased because of the forethought of his great-grandfather, William H. Cowles Sr., who established the company in 1891. Ultimately the strongest advantage he sees with his independent ownership model is not having to play by the same rules publicly owned companies do. "I always think we're small enough, agile enough to make changes quickly, and we're big enough to make a difference in terms of our own market and even on a national scale," he said. In terms of the quality of journalism, he said he sometimes thinks that quality means less to people today because everyone is moving so quickly and communities are so transient. "But I still think there is a core group in every community that are the movers and shakers and the people who stay there and have the best interest of the community at heart. Those are the people we most serve and that really depend on us."

The Cowles company board is made up of Cowles, who serves as president and runs the print division; his sister, Elizabeth A. "Betsy" Cowles, chairman and vice president, who oversees the television station, insurance agency, and real estate holdings; and Steven R. Rector, chief financial officer. Betsy and Stacey's uncle, Jim Cowles, manages the newsprint and timber operations. As for the fifth generation and whether they will be willing to step up to run the company, Cowles said it's too early to know. He and his sister have four children, the oldest of whom is fifteen. There is a chance that one or more of them will be interested, he said. "We're in a constant process of educating the next generation about the significance of our legacy here and the importance of the newspaper and the media," as well as the significant role the newspaper has played in the community, he said. "We derive our sense of purpose really from the media business, and we try to explain what that's all about to the next generation." Cowles said the newspaper's role is to be "a steward of the community. We believe first and foremost that we're here to reflect the community and help it understand what's going on."[3]

Different Company Culture

For Davis, the biggest advantage of being family owned is the reinvestment the family makes in the company, including capital improvements in facilities and new technology. Cowles and his family put a great deal of money back into the company, Davis said. He notices the difference when he visits other newspapers. "It's just kind of a different corporate culture—one that is less bottom-line driven," he said. The publisher has goals for financial returns, and the newspaper participates in the Inland Cost and Revenue Study so they know what other newspapers their size are producing. "We know the basic benchmarks," Davis said, "and we do the best we can to shoot at those. But we also recognize that we don't have some of the advantages of economies of scale that you would get from a corporate office for support services. The publisher takes that into consideration when he sets the goals."

Ultimately, though, the publisher doesn't look from quarter to quarter but rather longer term. "We don't have to satisfy investors on a quarterly basis. The stock is not publicly traded, so the investors, the family, doesn't really take the pulse like you would see normal investors do." That mindset, and the lack of a general manager at the *Spokesman-Review*, makes Cowles a hands-on manager, Davis said. He has a passion for having a good newspaper, for serving the community, and for producing a fair return. Quality is key. "We want to be the best newspaper of our size in the country," Davis said, so all decisions support that goal.[4]

Of course, there is a high cost associated with keeping up high quality both in the product and the workplace. Cowles said the company is heavily invested in its facilities. "We're technologically a terrific place to work," he said. People need to have the tools they need to do their jobs. "I don't want to work in a dingy, dark building with a seven-year-old computer. I want to have what I need to get the job done, and I want my people to have what they need, too," he said, acknowledging that there have been cutbacks in capital spending in the last ten years. "I think we've gotten smarter about what we're spending on. I think that's one of the things we can control better than chain papers who have absolute rules, strict rules about what you're going to spend and who you have to go to" when making those decisions.

Production Manager Paul Schafer, who has been at the newspaper for more than thirty years, said the paper has grown smaller. "While we still have good-size papers on Saturday and Sunday comparably, we have some pretty lean papers earlier in the week." He said he is alarmed that circulation is dropping in their home county. In outlying areas, however, it has stayed steady.[5]

Like publicly owned newspapers, the company does have budgets and holds managers accountable for meeting targets. Bonus plans have been focused on the numbers, something Cowles said he wants to change because it leads to shorter-term thinking. "We don't want to make decisions that will benefit us in one year and cause us a problem the next year," he said.

Staff size at the *Spokesman-Review* has shrunk, just like at most newspapers. Across the company in 2006 there were about 590 full-time employees compared to 720 in 1992, Cowles said.[6] Davis said when revenues slip, reality kicks in and companies realize that costs have to be contained, but the way a company goes about cutting staff makes a big difference. "Cutting back staff is an exercise in focus," he said, because it makes you determine the things that are most important. The result is a more efficient and perhaps better company. The downside, however, is a loss of job security and loyalty. Forced layoffs can be devastating, and seizing the opportunity to lower numbers through attrition is definitely the way to go. The *Spokesman-Review* hasn't always practiced that philosophy, especially in the newsroom, which had been immune to cuts for years. "In my opinion, we had every opportunity to do more of it through attrition. I think it would have had much less impact on morale," Davis said.[7]

Former Editor Steve Smith, who came to the newspaper about five years ago after working for other family owned newspapers, Freedom Newspapers, Gannett, and Knight Ridder, said he has taken about 25 positions out of the newsroom. In 2002–2001 there were 167 people in the newsroom. But after two rounds of buyouts, he now has about 124 full-time permanent positions. He acknowledges that more cutbacks may be down the road. One way to do that is simply to hold positions "dark" or unfilled. The industry for years has used staffing formulas tied to circulation numbers. Smith said it used to be 1.2 or 1.3 per thousand circulation. "When I look at my staff, if we were a Gannett paper, based on my experience with Gannett and our current circulation, instead of 124 full-time permanents, I'd probably be somewhere in the

105–110 range. If I were a Knight Ridder paper, maybe 112–115," he said. "I know I'm well staffed by industry standards, but I have to get a little closer." As far as salaries go, he said the journalists at the *Spokesman-Review* are still better off than the average journalist elsewhere in the industry. He said he keeps journalists motivated by focusing on core values—reminding them that they are there for a reason. "We do good work because we're called to do good work. And when we operate at our best, we perform a meaningful public service," he said. It's important to hire people in the organization who share those commitments and values and create a culture in which those things are supported and sustained.[8]

Schafer said the newspaper has lost 135 full-time positions since 2000. He said layoffs are harder at family owned newspapers than at those controlled by outside shareholders and distant corporate bosses. "It's a lot easier for someone to send a directive that you need twenty fewer people on Friday," he said. "It's a lot harder when you know them and your kids play soccer together. I think we dragged our feet for awhile here." One of the challenges is if you're going to reduce personnel, you have to reduce some of the workload.

The newspaper has three editions every night. "We run Idaho, Spokane Valley, and Spokane," Cowles said. And there are three bureaus—one in Coeur d'Alene, one in the Spokane Valley, and one downtown. "We aren't zoning daily ROP* advertising for the city or the valley. We do zone for Idaho," he said. In Spokane County, there is a zoned product called the *Voice*. There's a *South Voice* and a *Valley Voice*. There is also a product called *Handle Extra*. The publisher said part of the *Spokesman-Review*'s circulation decline was intentional because economically it was too difficult to maintain. "We had probably one of the biggest geographic branches for a paper our size in the country," something traditionally known as vanity circulation. "We have always felt that covering the 5th Congressional District was the area we wanted to serve, but we're down to not quite covering the whole fifteen counties." The newspaper covers about a dozen counties in eastern Washington and five counties in north Idaho. "It's difficult to cover that broad region with news coverage, and it's certainly expensive to drive papers out more than two hours to reach people," Cowles said.[9] In mid-2007, the *Spokesman-Review* posted a daily circulation of about 93,000 and Sunday circulation of about 118,000.[10]

Another cost saving initiative at the *Spokesman-Review* was decreasing the size of the newspaper, including going to a fifty-inch web and cutting news hole. Smith said the paper historically tried to keep the advertising to news ratio in the 50:50 percent range. "We've been running somewhere between 52

---

*   ROP is an acronym for "run of paper" and refers to ads that can run anywhere they fit in the newspaper.

and 52.5 percent news to advertising," he said. But in 2006 Cowles asked him to exercise more budget discipline, so he cut the percentage from about 52.3 percent down to the 50.5–50.8 range. That is about 20 percent less than in 2005 and translates into a savings of about one thousand pages of news hole a year, he said. The cuts were made across the board, in every section of the newspaper. Smith isn't willing to say that cutbacks don't harm the news product. "We have to be honest with ourselves and with our readers that we are providing less. Yes, we can make smarter decisions, but I can't argue that the paper as a whole is better today than it was a year ago or two years ago," he said.

The tough decisions he has to make and the current economic climate for newspapers are enormously challenging for Smith. "Every day, every week gets harder," he said. "Being editor is harder than I think it's ever been, here or anywhere else." But while stressful, his said his work is different at the *Spokesman-Review*. "The problem with Gannett was that the bureaucracy was such that I was spending 60–80 percent of my time on strategic planning paperwork. You'd do a massive strategic plan for somebody at corporate, and then somebody else at corporate would come along and say, 'No, our initiative this year is features, so you've got to redo it.' " Smith said he wrote five plans in two years while at the *Statesman-Journal* in Salem, Oregon, and downsized the newsroom by more than 25 percent in two years, at "a paper where our profit margin was running 40–45 percent." In Spokane, the paperwork and bureaucracy issues are nonexistent, and the budgeting process is simple. "My strategic plan is an Excel spreadsheet," he said. "At Gannett I had to manage my budget on a daily basis. Here I work on a monthly basis. If I was over twenty-five cents in Salem, I'd get a report on Friday telling me that I'd overspent my budget on Wednesday. It was amazing. That's how they do it. That's how they maintain that fiscal discipline."

Smith said he doesn't think the corporate conglomerates have done much to help the quality of journalism, and like his peers, he subscribes to the theory that "you can't save your way to survival." He credits Cowles for being a terrific businessman. He said the publisher is striving for a level of profitability that is in the low mid-range for the industry as a whole. "What Stacey is able to do—and I honor him for this—is to compromise his financial goals in order to maintain some level of quality. But he can't do that indefinitely, and he can't do that alone." There are still other family members to answer to who expect a reasonable return on their investment.

Editorial Independence

Smith said he's fortunate to have a publisher who still allows him to make decisions that cost the company money. Despite the economic pressures that he's under, "I have the freedom to make decisions that offend advertisers. We go where the stories are," he said. One example was a story the newsroom did in 2005 about a federal investigation into one of the largest gun dealers in town. "The ATF* was investigating them for not doing the work that they're supposed to do when they sell guns," Smith said. The company was infuriated by the stories, pulled advertising for a while, changed their contract, and threatened to boycott. "And at no time did Stacey or Shaun Higgins, who manages the business side, ever come to me and say 'don't do this.' "

A couple of years earlier, a columnist offended Comcast by writing that their managers were a spawn of Satan. "It was hyperbolic," Smith said. "The problem with Comcast is that the founder and owner and his son are devout Christians. They're from Arkansas and they go to church every Sunday, and the column was highly critical. But what really pissed them off was the 'spawn of Satan' reference because they felt that was an attack on their personal integrity." They pulled their advertising, which hurt because Comcast is a big telecommunications advertiser. "Mostly we won them back, but I didn't have Stacey or Shaun in my office."

Finally, a regionally owned tire chain was upset because they thought the *Spokesman-Review* was ignoring them and their charitable giving. What really set them off, Smith said, was when they bought the naming rights to the Gonzaga Athletic Arena and had their name painted on the floor. When they went back and looked at pictures that had been published in the *Spokesman-Review* of Gonzaga basketball games, "they decided that we had deliberately taken pictures that obscured" their name on the floor. So they pulled their advertising. Smith said the editors tried to explain that photographers shooting basketball games are shooting players, not the floor. "But I didn't have Shaun or Stacey nipping at my heels. ... I've always been blessed with publishers who understand that kind of editorial independence, and Stacey is terrific on that."

Influence of Traditions

One of the family's challenges, Smith said, is sustaining their core business while developing the wherewithal to research and develop new initiatives. He said while the *Spokesman-Review* is spectacular on the news side, it is lagging on the business side when it comes to innovation. "We're not as aggressive as we might otherwise be on some of the kinds of things that we need to be doing. That's one thing where the corporates have beaten us," he said.[11]

Davis agrees that research and development, long lacking in the newspaper industry, is vital for the future. Coming from a computer and accounting

---

* ATF is an acronym for the Bureau of Alcohol, Tobacco, Firearms and Explosives, a law enforcement agency under the U.S. Department of Justice.

background, he said newspapers are a unique business model—a manufacturer with a very perishable product. "But we don't act like a manufacturer," he said. "We're so steeped in tradition and the way things have always been done—I think that haunts our industry." Newspapers traditionally don't think about research and development (R&D) or economies of scale. "We think about cost containment, and that's what's in the blinders of being a newspaper. I think it hurts our innovation."

With high production costs and high overhead, Davis said he's afraid circulation declines will end with a great deal of over-capacity. The question, he said, is: How do you leverage that over-capacity to produce new revenue? Niche products, the Internet, convergence have all been tried, but he doesn't think those are the only options. "If you think about it, people just want access to information on whatever device they use," be it cell phones, iPods, or personal digital assistant. "I think there are a lot more options and opportunities, and newspapers—not just family owned newspapers—but as a whole have been late investing in research and development. We're paying for that" now. Unlike other industries, when you look at newspaper budgets, there is no research and development allocation. And while the newspaper industry fortunately has had a long life cycle and papers have been very profitable, that stability is beginning to erode. "Now we're starting the downslope. In order to pull that out, you have to do something differently. That's what industries do," Davis said. Newspapers need to step up, recreate, and reinvent themselves. The *Spokesman-Review* has put aside some money for R&D rather than just trying one thing or another. But Davis said there needs to be more innovative thinking and a broader perspective. "Let's put that under the auspices of R&D and say, 'OK, let's have an R&D Department,' " he said. It would be an innovative approach.

Davis said newspapers believe they are a mass-market enterprise, but they really aren't. If you look at the statistics, there is a specific demographic that reads daily newspapers. "We try to kid ourselves that we're mass market, but based on what we put into content, we attract a certain type of reader," he said. That's not surprising given how journalists are trained, hired, and promoted. "Basically you lose some diversity of thought or ideas because journalists generally go to journalism school, are hired by people looking at other people who are like them, who write like them, who produce things like them," he said. The result is a disconnection between content and the potential for readers, leading to an increasingly fragmented and adversarial type of environment. "I don't have all the answers. I just know that there are certain hot buttons that the newspaper pushes and we lose readers." The *Spokesman-Review* accidentally left out the Jumble for a couple of days once, and Davis said he was amazed at the firestorm that omission created. "We're worried about hard news and you leave out something like the crossword puzzle or a comic or the Jumble, and it's amazing. This is just really strange."

Davis said he is a firm believer that readers are attracted to both news and advertising and that the newspaper needs to be the "go-to place" for readers in their market. "We need to be the connection between whatever information people want—whether it's news, advertising, whatever—we need to be the place to go," he said. That is what is going to drive revenue, and that is what advertisers want. "We need to have something so compelling that, if you live in Spokane, Washington, you have to come to us—either print or online—to get it." Newspapers are unique because they have not one customer base but two segments of customers that overlap. There are readers and advertisers. An advertiser is both a reader and an advertiser, but a reader is not always an advertiser. Understanding both is the key, Davis said.[12]

New Operating Models

Daniel Johnson, director of subscriber acquisition and retention at the *Spokesman-Review*, said that for years the industry focused only on gaining but not keeping subscribers. Ten or twenty years ago, the model was, "Let's not worry about retention," he said. "If we throw enough subscription sales against the wall and we can get them to stay on long enough, the circulation numbers will grow. But now you truly have to go out and market the newspaper as a product that brings value to people's lives."

Like many other newspapers, the *Spokesman-Review* partners with retailers such as Walmart to get shoppers to buy and subscribe. Sales crews attend trade shows and other events that attract enough potential readers. Then, once there, they cross-promote the print and the online products. Promoting sales through third-party bulk purchases by other companies also works. The *Spokesman-Review* has had limited success marketing to hotels because most are nationally owned chains whose corporate owners have negotiated with Gannett headquarters to distribute *USA TODAY* to their rooms. The solution for the *Spokesman-Review* was to print the breakfast menu door hangers that offer hotel guests a chance to check the newspaper they wanted delivered or give them a choice at check-in. Having the newspaper for sale at the desk downstairs is a given. It all comes down to branding, "making sure we are promoting full support of the *Spokesman-Review* brand," Johnson said. There are several publications published at the newspaper, and it's important that "one brand won't get in the way of the other."[13]

Among the niche products the *Spokesman-Review* has developed as part of their enhanced market coverage (EMC) is a weekly called *Pinch*, which Shaun O'L. Higgins, director of marketing and sales, calls "a little bit of everything."

In fact, the name *Pinch* means a pinch of everything. *Pinch* started out as *Food, Etc.* and was basically an envelope to carry grocery ads. It was renamed *Pinch* in July 2005, and when it was updated in October that year it was six pages. By March 2006, it had grown to sixteen, and Higgins expects it to reach twenty-four pages with 80 percent ads. *Food, Etc.* had nothing but duplicated *Spokesman-Review* content, "which was another reason not to buy the newspaper because you got the food section and all the food ads anyway," Higgins said. So they decided to revise the concept of *Pinch. Pinch* doesn't contain news and is not tied to the newsroom, but it is based on newsroom standards. "We do not write pieces from advertisers," Higgins said. But they do accept news releases, for instance, about a local company getting a national award. "It has to be something outstanding," he said. "I call it the 'not quite newspaper.' " It is delivered free to seventy-one thousand households that do not subscribe to the newspaper. Subscribers of the newspaper can get it without inserts because they already get inserts with the *Spokesman-Review.*

Another product, *Better Health and Living,* is part of a partnership with a group in Fort Lauderdale, Florida. The *Spokesman-Review* provides one local story, and the rest of the publication is compiled by the Florida editorial staff and then distributed to about fifty markets around the country. Higgins said the content is strong, slick, and it is targeted as a buy for businesses such as natural food stores and exercise equipment outlets. "It tends to be a kind of high-end publication, so we distribute it with the newspaper but only in higher-end ZIP codes—50,000 copies six times a year," he said. The *Spokesman-Review* sells ads for *Better Health and Living* and pays to have it printed. "They arrange for the printing, and then we take the profits in the end. They make their profits in the printing and production, and we make our profits on the advertising," Higgins said. It is moderately successful for the newspaper, and the readers who get it like it. "We think it probably has appeal to all of our readers, but it was just too expensive to consider a 100,000 paper rollout until we saw the ads themselves." Eventually, they said, they think they can raise the rates and expand circulation of the product, which is a small tabloid-size magazine on glossy stock focused on the twenty- to thirty-five-year-old market.

The newspaper also partners with others to produce a series of market real estate books, an apartment finder, and *Mature Living Choices.* The company signed a contract in 2006 to do an online auction. The *Spokesman-Review* provides the advertising and promotion for merchandise, then sells the merchandise online and uses the proceeds to pay for the ads. The newspaper runs three community sales events a year in which they sell booths. Two are community-wide garage sales and one is a career fair. They also sell a package of booths and convention planning services as well as newspaper advertising as a package, and promote those to the community. They always get a great turnout, Higgins said.

There is a full range of special sections every year—about twenty on the special sections calendar including golf and hunting guides. Companies that Care is a section designed for companies to publish their community profile as an advertorial and to buy a facing page of advertising. These sections are all done by the Marketing Department and outside the newsroom. "Again, the standard here is 'not quite news,' " Higgins said.

The newspaper owned a TV book company called Print Marketing Concepts for ten years. Based in Houston, the company brokered the listing through a Dallas company, did production, and in some cases printed the books, which it then sold to seventy newspapers around the country. But "we sold it to its employees at the beginning of the year [2006]. It was just too much trouble for the return," Higgins said.

While some newspapers offer limited free classified ads, the *Spokesman-Review* has a different take on building classified revenue. Higgins explains: If you buy a classified ad in the *Spokesman-Review* that is going to run three or four days, you may pay, for example, $35. So while the buyer is on the phone, the staffer says, "For $3.25 we'll give you an additional seventy-five thousand households in our nonsubscriber product," meaning in *Pinch*. It's a flat rate; no matter how big the ad is, it will run in *Pinch* for an additional $3.25, and 90 percent of the people on the other end of the phone say yes. The result meant going from zero pages of classifieds in *Pinch* to six pages. "The subtlety is the easiest thing in the world," Higgins said, "because you spent $35 already and you think seventy thousand households for an additional $3.25. Gee, I'm smart." It's a decision that's small enough that the buyer thinks they can make it and feel like a smart shopper. "It's a really good buy. We don't want things to just sound like good buys; they have to be good buys. And they have to make people feel smart because they decided to take advantage of that offer. ... We've had phenomenal success with it. It's not quite free, but it's cheap."

Other changes include increasing the size of the type in classifieds. It's simple, and everybody likes it regardless of age. "So we get less revenue per page? I can't take revenue per page to the bank if nobody reads these classifieds," Higgins said. Customers are not going to buy an ad if the type is so small they can't read it or if they don't like the look of it. Type size for classifieds in the *Spokesman-Review* has gone from 6 point to 7.5 point. The next change is moving from a ten-column format to six columns. The same strategy used to pitch *Pinch* applies. Higgins said the plan is to make the classified format the same as the retail format so they can do more cross-promotion. If someone wants to put an ad in classifieds because they want someone who is looking for a job to see it, the staff can offer to place it in retail as a way to target those who aren't looking in classifieds. "We tell them: 'Place your ad in the classifieds and we'll pick it up on the same day or the next day in retail.' " The second ad is 50 percent the cost of the first one. The same is true if someone wants to place an ad in retail. "We say, 'You really ought to run that in the classifieds. We can give you an extra day's run on it, or you can run two on the same day and reach the maximum audience.' " It's a new approach.[14]

From a circulation standpoint, it's all about customer service. Johnson said the *Spokesman-Review*'s delivery standard is to deliver the newspaper where the customer wants it—on the porch, behind the front door, or in a tube or box. "We don't go down the street throwing them in the driveways and the yards," he said. The result is fewer than the average number of complaints.[15] The industry average is about two daily per one thousand customers. The *Spokesman-Review* gets about one. Bagging the paper is expensive for newspapers and is not required but encouraged on wet days. "We get very few complaints about papers being delivered in poor condition," Higgins said.[16] All carriers are over age eighteen. About 95 percent of subscriptions are prepaid with a goal of moving as close to 100 percent as possible, Johnson said. Home delivery makes up about 85 percent of total circulation, and single-copy sales run about 12–13 percent. An online subscription of the *Spokesman-Review* is $7. The print edition is $14.50 a month. Daily single-copy sales are $0.50, and Sunday editions sell for $1.50.

Johnson said the *Spokesman-Review* has revamped the Circulation Department to move to a team-based approach from a hierarchal structure. "Basically my marching orders are to figure out a way to maintain circulation and to stop the downward spiral. ... If we could level off, maintain a good core, I think that's the key."[17]

New Media Opportunities

Cowles said the company's vision for the future is to deliver news and advertising to the local market in the form and at the time that people want it. That means envisioning everything related to new technology. "We pretty quickly figured out how to use the Internet as a distribution channel," he said. And the paper has seized on the web as a new medium, too. There are at least thirty blogs up and running, which generates much online traffic. From the start, the online operation was integrated into the newsroom operation. Cowles said he believes that when new technology becomes available, people cut back on the way they use other media, "so our philosophy has been to take advantage of the new medium and make adjustments as we go along." He said the new medium creates a new realm of activity and expands the market to some extent. "But you have to weigh that expansion of the market versus your share of the new market."

In Spokane, convergence is called cooperation. Because the company owns KHQ-TV, there is cross-promotion and some sharing of content. But because a TV station and a newspaper are such different kinds of media and because they have different views on how to cover a story, it's been a challenge. "You can't just plug that together," Cowles said.[18]

With the large number of blogs, Smith calls the *Spokesman-Review* "the blog paper of all time ... the national voice for blogging as journalists." He said the newsroom is trying to avoid setting formal criteria for blogs because much of what is being done is experimental. "We have no problem with this staff exploring new and different ways of delivering information. It's very bold and aggressive, and I'm proud of them."[19]

Higgins said in addition to SpokesmanReview.com, there is another website called Spokane.net that is a community-based site. Geared to any age user, Spokane.net offers weather, headlines, and a place where consumers can send in their favorite pictures, perhaps of a sunset or a night at the beach. "We have 80 percent male users on SpokesmanReview.com," Higgins said. But Spokane. net has turned out to be much more appealing to women even though it wasn't designed specifically for them. "We were surprised that this audience developed that way." Spokane.net also links to an electronic version of *Pinch*. The site uses community software that allows users to post things like minutes of Scout meetings or to share information among their small group.

Focus On Results

The team approach starts at the top at the *Spokesman-Review*. Higgins said the newspaper has a very active ownership group. While it is family owned, there is no less pressure to run a company that is well managed and performing within a range of industry standards. A publisher even at a family held company is responsible for the bottom line. "He has to sell the idea that the value of their holdings are increasing every year in some way, that the company is growing, that they won't wake up one morning and find that they don't have a valuable asset," Higgins said. He said he likes working for the Cowles family. "They show up for work every day, and that really impresses me. And they do have their heart in quality." He said the core of the company's investments, the family traditions, have been in strong, viable businesses. "Not an obsession with money, but to run clean, honest, decent businesses that produce papers that provide a public service, and to produce them at a profit." He said the owners are good people. "If there's ever anybody that deserved to own a newspaper it's the Cowles."[20]

In late 2007, the *Spokesman-Review* began eliminating jobs through layoffs and retirements as part of a company-wide cost-savings strategy. Smith resigned as editor in October 2008 when the newspapers announced additional cuts. Gary Graham, who had served as managing editor, replaced him.

Notes

1   W. Stacey Cowles (publisher, *Spokesman-Review*), interview with the author, March 24, 2006.
2   Robert Davis (business manager, *Spokesman-Review*), interview with the author, March 24, 2006.
3   Cowles, interview.
4   Davis, interview.
5   Paul Schafer (production manager, *Spokesman-Review*), interview with the author, March 24, 2006.
6   Cowles, interview.
7   Davis, interview.
8   Steve Smith (former editor, *Spokesman-Review*), interview with the author, March 24, 2006.
9   Cowles, interview.
10 Cowles.
11 Smith, interview.
12 Davis, interview.
13 Daniel Johnson (director, subscriber acquisition and retention, *Spokesman-Review*), interview with the author, March 24, 2006.
14 Shaun O'L. Higgins (director, marketing and sales, *Spokesman-Review*), interview with the author, March 24, 2006.
15 Johnson, interview.
16 Higgins, interview.
17 Johnson, interview.
18 Cowles, interview.
19 Smith, interview.
20 Higgins, interview.

6

The Register-Guard

When Alton Baker Sr., thirty-three, arrived by train in Eugene, Oregon, from Cleveland with his wife and four children on March 1, 1927, he couldn't have known that he would begin a publishing legacy that would last eighty years. Alton had long wanted to own a newspaper. His chance came when he acquired the *Guard*, which was founded in 1867.

In a history of the *Guard*, published on March 3, 2002, to celebrate the Bakers' seventy-five-year ownership, Bob Welch writes that after three years of intense competition with the *Eugene City Register*, Alton Sr. purchased the *Register* on November 17, 1930 and combined the two papers to create the *Eugene Register-Guard*. Bunky Baker, Alton Sr.'s son, became managing editor in 1950. His brother, Ted, was named director of advertising in 1951. On March 1, 1961, Alton Sr. named Bunky publisher and Ted general manager. Alton Sr. died on October 26, 1961.

Under Bunky and Ted's leadership, the newspaper became known for its outstanding journalism and won a number of awards including the Oregon Newspaper Publishers Association's general excellence competition, thirteen out of twenty years during the 1970s and 1980s.

In 1983 the paper moved to morning publication, following a national trend, and dropped "Eugene" from its name, becoming the *Register-Guard*.

Securing the newspaper's future has long been on the minds of family members, from the five of Generation II to the sixteen members of Generation III and the twenty-nine members of Generation IV. After months of meetings on the future of the *Guard* in 1986, the tradition that had forged the family legacy prevailed. Welch writes: "In December, Generation III presented a letter to their forebears with two major themes: First, they were appreciative of the legacy that was being offered them. Second, they'd like to continue it."[1]

In 1987, Tony Baker, Bunky's son became publisher and president of Guard Publishing Company. His cousin, Fletcher Little, son of Louise Baker Little, became general manager and vice president of the company. Bunky retired and Ted became chairman of the board.[2]

The New Guard

The new leaders faced labor struggles, the need for a new production facility and press, and sweeping technological innovations and cultural changes that would plunge newspapers around the country into a downward spiral. But the story is fundamentally different in Eugene and one that may give the Bakers a brighter future.

Tony said that he believes intensely in the value of independently owned newspapers. The pressures to remain a strong business are internal, not from far-flung stockholders and a distant corporate office. "We live and die by our own decisions here," he said. "We're pretty close to the ground. We know our territory. We hope we know what's in the hearts and minds of our readers. We know the advertising climate."[3] But the true advantage of being locally owned is the fact that the owners live and work there and have a real sense of community. A long-term publisher who has ties to a community, rather than one who works for a publicly owned media conglomerate and spends two or three years in a city before moving on to the next assignment, makes a huge difference. "We care about what happens here," he said. "Our bosses, in many respects, are our readers and advertisers, and there is a public trust. We're working on behalf of our readers. And I'm not sure that's the same motivation and why you come to work every day if you're a publisher of a publicly held paper. I think they have different marching orders."

Readers in Eugene, the publisher said, have a feeling of ownership of the newspaper and are not shy about letting the Bakers know what they think about the job the family does. The family, too, is clear about its mission "to be intensely local." Baker said, "If we lose sight of that, shame on us because that is what we do. We're not the *Wall Street Journal*; we're not the *Washington Post*; we're not the *New York Times*. We're the *Register-Guard*, and our bread and butter is taking care of minding the store on all things local."[4]

Fletcher Little, former *Guard* vice president who left the newspaper in 2007, said he thinks the primary advantage of being family owned is that the owners make decisions for themselves right there in Eugene and all of the owners are family members. "Our profit margins need to be strong enough to support the business, but it's not a huge demand, like a public company might be," to keep the profit margins high to attract more investors. The key advantage is being nimble and quick to make decisions. Agreeing with the publisher, Little said because the owners all live and work in the community and don't move from one newspaper to another, one company to another, or one community to another, they have deep roots. "I think that serves us well," he said. "Most people that we do business with are aware that we're locally owned, and I think that works in our favor."[5]

There are negatives, however, including limited room for employee advancement at the company. That could be a deterrent to attracting talented staff, along with the fact that there is far less turnover than at a publicly owned newspaper. But, Little said, some people want to come to Eugene to work for a family owned business. "There is a different dynamic that enters the picture than simply working for a public company," he said. "It just adds another dimension to managing a company. I don't know if it's better or worse than a public company and having thousands of stockholders, but it's different."

The lack of resources, theoretically available at big corporations, could be considered a disadvantage. Little said sometimes he and other family members lament not having the deep pockets of conglomerates. But, at the same time, "We don't have to go to a parent corporation to finance whatever we think we want to do. We've been fortunate that we've always been able to finance whatever venture we wanted to pursue."

One example is an expansion that came in the late 1980s and early 1990s, a time when the national economy was slowing. The press at the *Guard* was getting old, and replacement parts were difficult to find. "We knew if an irreplaceable part broke down, we'd be out of business," Little said. So they invested in a new press and a building to house it when the rest of the country was in a recession. He said there were articles in *Editor & Publisher* saying, "What do these people know that we don't?" What the Bakers knew was that they had to do it to keep going. "It was our decision, and we found the money to do it. We had full control over our destiny."

Little believes that when a local paper is bought by a big conglomerate, people in the community do notice a difference. There are simple reasons. New owners tend not to put as many resources into the local product, rates tend to increase, and the company runs much leaner with fewer employees. Sometimes the benefits aren't quite as good, creating an atmosphere where employees come and go. He said he's sure the community would notice if the *Guard* were not independently owned.[6]

Tough Times

Being local, however, doesn't insulate the *Guard* from the same struggles facing all newspapers today. It's a painful time with declining ad revenues, the loss of major advertisers, and rising production costs. The *Guard* lost one of its biggest retail advertisers in 2006. The difference in Eugene is that the paper's response to turbulent times is based on the philosophy of the local owners. "As long as we can have it [the newspaper] viable and maintain the integrity of the news product, we're going to be much better off," Tony said. "You can't save your way to prosperity. I absolutely believe that. ... But right now I think the prudent thing is to tighten things."[7]

That tightening has led to a smaller news hole and fewer pages in the newspaper's sections. "We've had a budget of round figures—60 percent news hole," Tony said. "But we've ratcheted that down to 41–59, 42–58. To ratchet down really makes a dramatic difference in the paper. It sounds incremental in terms of percentage, but it makes a big difference." He said those figures are over a seven-day average, that Monday and Tuesday papers are below 40 percent, but the Sunday and weekend papers are much higher. "Other ways to control newsprint is in your shopper, your total market coverage piece. We've tightened that from twelve pages to ten pages because it's pretty easy to do" and there is flexibility in the number of copies produced and where they are sent, he said. But if you cut the news product too much, people will notice.

With the shrinking news hole, there also have been staff positions left unfilled and layoffs. But, Tony said, "It takes x number of people to put the product out and do it seven days a week, 365 days a year." They also look for ways to develop new revenue streams. "That's real important to us. Again, we can't save our way to prosperity, so we've got to look at other things." Rather than sending the revenue from new products to outside stockholders, at the *Guard* it is reinvested in the business. "Our philosophy is, when we do better, we put the money back into the product to enhance it further. That's the future. That's been our legacy, and that's the same philosophy going forward."[8]

In mid-2006 the *Guard* was in a "selective hiring freeze." Little said some positions are what he calls "mission critical." When employees leave, the company is careful about which ones are replaced, and there have been a few layoffs. Most staff cuts have occurred through attrition. He said in 2005 the company had about 430 employees. By mid-2006 there were about 400. "We're definitely operating leaner than we did. It's certainly more difficult, but we've tried to do it strategically so that one department doesn't bear the brunt of the attrition," he said.[9]

In the Newsroom

What does it mean in the newsroom to be independently owned? Managing Editor Dave Baker said he has a great deal of autonomy and only one person to go to for decisions on news coverage. "I've good a pretty good ear, and he's my cousin," Dave said.[10] "There aren't a whole lot of committees or red tape or anything else that I have to go through as a managing editor in order to do the right thing journalistically." Because Dave is a member of the family that owns the paper, "I know what the mission of the family is. And the mission is we're going to put out a good newspaper." He said there is a sense of pride that motivates the family.

Being close and involved in the community is valuable for a managing editor, he said. "For people to know that I'm plugged into the community and care about it overall is a very positive thing. I have a vested interest in the community both from a social perspective as well as an economical one. I think that people figure that out."

Like other managing editors, Dave sometimes has to deal with advertiser pressures. He cited a story the *Guard* did about a fraud lawsuit involving a car dealership that led to the dealership pulling its advertising for two or three months. The newspaper got some pressure and some criticism, but "Tony is rock solid on stuff like that," he said. It's worth remembering that Tony came to the publisher's seat through the news ranks. Advertiser pressures still have an impact, but Dave said, "I think overall we probably do better than most papers when it comes to independence from advertising pressure."

The paper has changed over the years. Like many independents, fiscal accountability has been a more recent development. Dave said when he started at the paper twenty years ago, he didn't think they even had a newsroom budget. "We had an accountant who kind of oversaw the whole business and spending, and if you wanted something you went to him and he often said, 'OK,' " It's different now. There is more scrutiny about staffing and news coverage. "Of course we have shareholders, but the family pretty much runs the board here, so there isn't a great cry from the shareholders to say, 'We've got to make a lot more money.' "

The newsroom is feeling financial pressures, however. In 2006 for the first time in the newspaper's history, an ad was placed on the cover of *TV Week*. The *Guard* is now charging for obits beyond the brief death notices that are free.

Staff tightening has cost the newsroom nearly a dozen positions in three years, including reporters, a team leader, and a copy editor. "When it comes to payroll, we're way above average. But that's mostly because we pay people more, and we have really good benefits. But in terms of the number of bodies in the newsroom, I think we're now a little below average," Dave said.

There has been tightening in news hole, including in sports, local, business, and briefs. The newspaper has been revamped to add more color section fronts. There has been talk about trimming stock pages and making changes in the TV schedule listings because of reader usage, and additional ways for readers to get stocks and TV schedule information. Dave said he thinks the days are numbered for those features because of the amount of newsprint devoted to stocks and TV schedules and the lack of advertising in those sections.

Where the *Guard* has made strides is in revamped features sections. Sunday is a Life section, Monday for the 20 Below age group, Tuesday is Outdoors, Wednesday is the Entrée food section, Thursday is Arts, and Friday is Ticket, the weekly entertainment section. Saturday is the *TV Week*. The 20 Below section, started more than ten years ago, is written by high school students and edited by the features editor. Dave said there is talk of revamping that section into one targeted to women and focusing on family life, daycare, childrearing, home life, and counseling. The 20 Below section would be folded into the new section. "We've done a little bit of inside-the-company asking women what they think of it, and it's been really well received," he said.

But the crucial question, Dave said, is how newspapers are going to survive. "The lines don't seem to be going in the right way on the fever charts when it comes to market share and the revenue it's going to take to continue to provide the staff to put out a good paper. That's what we're experiencing right now." He suggests that more resources should be put into developing websites at newspapers because the "eyeballs are going to the Internet." He is looking for a light at the end of the tunnel. Part of the strategy, he said, "is just to hang on in hopes that people are going to need newspapers, whether it's on the Internet or wherever. We're going to survive and get through it. ... But when you see the news hole shrink and you lose reporters, it starts to scare you a bit."[11]

In Production

For Jerry LaCamp, production manager who has been at the *Guard* for more than thirty-eight years, being family owned means less red tape and quicker spending decisions without a long tedious wait for action from off-site executives. He senses that most *Guard* employees have a stronger sense of pride and loyalty to the owners than they would have if they worked for a public company. The reason, he said, is because the Bakers are willing to plow resources back into the newspaper. He described two types of production employee incentive plans designed to reward workers for doing their jobs to the best of their abilities. In the pressroom, a press operator can earn up to four dollars additionally a day for meeting deadlines and keeping quality and waste at acceptable levels. "It's based on four points, and they get the money if they stay through the end of the payout period. That encourages them to stay," LaCamp said.[12]

In distribution, an incentive plan awards workers for being on time, meeting cleanliness and waste standards, and participating in an exercise program designed to help them keep from getting hurt on the job. "They feed hoppers and things like that, and it's real stressful on their arms and wrists, so we started this program several years ago. Since then, the number of injuries we've had is down considerably," he said. Benefit packages at the *Guard* are, LaCamp believes, as good or better than at most other newspapers. "When we built this facility, one of the things that they put in was an exercise facility," he said.

Exempt employees have MBOs (management by objective plans), a practice started about ten years ago. "I think most people at that level would do whatever is necessary to get the job done anyway. It's a way to reward people when things are good," LaCamp said.

Family owned newspapers can be isolated from new industry technology. But going to trade shows can help production managers stay current. LaCamp said he looks for new equipment at trade shows. "We're not on the leading edge, but we're certainly not on the trailing edge of technology either," he said. The *Guard* is running lighter weight paper on its press than most newspapers. "Three years ago the standard was 30 pound, and we were running 27.7 pound. Now that probably is the standard throughout the industry, and we're running 26.5." He acknowledged that there is some curling, but "all of it curls. Maybe [it's] a little bit worse because it's got one thickness of fiber gone, but I would say our product is no worse than most newspapers out there."

He said the company does some outside printing jobs, but because most commercial advertisers want products that are different sizes than their press is capable of producing, outside jobs come along only a couple of times a month. Of course, if opportunities for commercial printing jobs come along "that will fit in the windows that we have and we could be competitive, absolutely we would do that." The company isn't specifically seeking outside printing jobs because the press simply is designed to be a newspaper press, he said.

Being locally owned and having a publisher who came up through the editorial ranks helps the newspaper set realistic deadlines for the news portion, LaCamp said. The paper goes to press at 12:30 a.m. daily, allowing the staff to get in the latest news—including sports stories and scores. Having a paper that's outdated is of no value to anyone, he said. In early 2006 the *Guard* went to a collect run from a straight run.[13] In a straight run, every time the press completes one revolution, two newspapers are produced; whereas, in a collect run, one newspaper is produced.[14] The result was big savings in press and distribution labor. "When we were running straight, it required us to sometime have preruns. Then you have to put the two products together, so you have extra labor in distribution," he said. "Running collect, you can cut the number of plates in half. Big, big savings. And then you cut your staffing. It just requires fewer bodies to produce a collect run than it does a straight run."

Additionally, inserts are done in-house from the point the paper is printed. Carriers are only required to insert a package into the Sunday paper. "But we precount all bundles," he said. Some newspapers tell advertisers they don't take inserts because of the costs involved. "We tell them, 'What do you want, and we'll try to do it,' " LaCamp said.[15]

In Circulation

From a circulation point of view, family ownership in Eugene means the Bakers, and especially the publisher, are very concerned about their standing in the community and that they provide a quality product, said Charles Downing, circulation director. "The publisher has said many times that this is a newspaper with a capital *N*. And saying that, he means he wants to provide the best newspaper possible and be the place where the public goes for information and advertising," Downing said.[16] The footprint of the *Guard* is about 10,000 square miles, and delivery is to about 4,700 miles a day. The company looks realistically about where it can afford to circulate and where it makes the most sense, he said. Ultimately they are profitable everywhere they circulate. "We have a template we use to determine profitability, which includes the preprint revenue that the Advertising Department gets. And in virtually every case, the circulation profit alone pays for us to be there. Maybe it's not hugely profitable, but when you add in the preprint revenue, it is. We analyze that about once a year."

Downing said about 94 percent of circulation is prepaid, with the other 6 percent collected by the carriers. The *Guard* does promotions at local coffee shops and fast-food outlets, including Burger King, McDonald's, and Starbucks, and in front of Walmarts. When it comes to promotions, "we try virtually everything we know," he said, including having salespeople standing in storefronts, using door-to-door soliciting teams, and setting up sales tables at local colleges. The carriers sell and so do the district managers. He said they have a "retention team internally, and their whole job is to call people back that are about to expire or have just expired their subscription and to try to get them back in the fold." The *Guard* also uses direct mail and subscription cards in single copies and sets up at fairs and special events. Several years ago, Downing started a Newspaper in Education program, which not only helps get paid circulation but, he hopes, recruits a new generation of readers. The *Guard* is also distributed in local hotels.

Do-not-call lists have taken a big toll on subscription sales. Downing said about 60 percent of the numbers the *Guard* could have called are now on the Do-Not-Call list. "We wiped out a pretty large number of our potential calls" when telemarketing restrictions were passed. Before that, telemarketing accounted for about 40 percent of new orders, he said, consistent with the percentage of new orders written at newspapers across the nation. Now it's about 30 percent. "We're frankly pleased with that because we were concerned that it would wipe us out completely," he said. The key is if your part-time telemarketing staff can get in and write orders and supplement their basic income with commissions. Then they will be happy enough to come back tomorrow and keep doing it. "We weren't sure they would, but in fact, they've managed to maintain."

Like many independents, the *Guard* porches the newspaper—to about 80 percent of its subscribers. The porch is the preferred place, Downing said.

There are also many newspaper tubes in the area because of the rain. But he said his policy has been that the newspaper is porched unless the subscriber says it's OK to deliver it somewhere else. "If we aren't porching it and someone calls to complain to me, I tell my managers, 'Make the customer happy.' We're not like power and light anymore. We can't just say, 'You have to have us.' "

About 95 percent of *Guard* carriers are adults, with only junior dealers left in outlying towns. Downing said about seventy out of one hundred staff are part-time, a ratio typical of most newspaper circulation departments. When staff cuts started about three years ago, the newspaper was in the process of changing its carrier model to adult carriers. "When we went to adult, we moved our district managers to an early morning shift and eliminated some support staff. We saved probably half a million dollars in both payroll and other expenses. It actually worked pretty well," he said. Since then, the depart-ment has tried to further refine its operation. "We're at the tail end of a trend that a lot of newspapers started following in the late 1990s where they realized that the most expensive delivery system is youth and junior dealers with a lot of kids and a lot of supervisors," he said. "I studied it for about ten years and noticed that every time papers did that and then tried to make all of it office pay, they'd lose about 10 percent of their circulation. ... So we made the change and didn't lose anything."[17]

Strategies For the Future

Like many newspapers, the *Guard* is focusing on developing niche products and expanding its Internet presence. One of eighteen new sections is a fly fishing section aimed at a specific audience. It is distributed to about twenty thousand and targeted to geographic areas that are more affluent and those for whom fly fishing is a pastime. In addition to reaching readers, smaller advertis-ers can take advantage of the niche products to reach their potential customers. A wine section called Tastings is designed to appeal to roughly the same group. Generations is a section aimed at the fifty-five and older demographic.

Little said the targeted sections are part of a broader strategy to bring in smaller advertisers. "These targeted sections are very compatible with a lower out-of-pocket cost, and from our perspective higher cost per thousand. Perhaps incrementally [it's] more profitable than any other business that we do, but it's smaller dollars," he said. "If we lose an account that spends a quarter million dollars a year with us, it takes an awful lot of those smaller advertisers to make up the difference. But if the profit margin is significantly higher, it's a lot easier for us to continue to do that kind of business."

In addition, the *Guard* changed its advertising rates in the mid-1990s. The paper had a three-tiered advertising pricing structure where Monday and

Tuesday had the lowest price, Wednesday and Thursday had the middle price, and the weekend had the highest price. Today that plan has evolved into a two-tiered structure. The premium is on Friday, Saturday, and Sunday because those are days with the highest circulation. Prices on Monday through Thursday are lower. "We also have single-copy sales that are higher on Saturday and Sunday. The advertisers get more for their buck on the weekend, and so we charge more for that," Little said. Ultimately the owners realized they were pricing smaller advertisers out of the newspaper and they needed to do something to remedy that. They could potentially raise prices if circulation on one day is up and lower prices if it is down on one day.

Being independent allows the company to make those changes that are unique to the Eugene market. Little said one value of being independent is that local advertisers can talk to the newspaper owners to be sure they are getting the best value for their advertising dollars.

Little sees geographically targeted publications as a trend, citing some newspapers that deliver their main product to surrounding bedroom communities miles away with a special community news section wrapped around it. There may be some potential for that strategy in Eugene along the Oregon Coast, he said. There are ways to create zoned pages or sections at a fairly low cost, but it's not a part of the *Guard*'s current strategic plan.

Enhancing the newspaper's Internet presence, however, is one of the company's most important initiatives. The newspaper had been updating its Internet edition at noon to keep from cannibalizing the print edition, Little said. Then the decision was made to move it earlier because research showed the website had less of a detrimental effect on the print product. They realized that it was their brand and another way to grow readership. "If we add the unique readers or users that go to our website who do not read the print product, our circulation—our readership more specifically—is in fact growing. So that's a very positive sign," he said. The financial strategy has been to offer the website with the current edition for free but to charge for access to archives more than one week old. The plans for the future will be to charge for some types of access, Little said, including e-mail service that will send headlines and hot links to readers who sign up. Receiving content on cell phones is in the future.

Looking Ahead

Twenty years ago, the newspaper reading habit started for many when they reached their mid-twenties and grew stronger until they reached age seventy, Little said. But today, readership of the print product probably starts in the mid-thirties. Pouring resources into the online product makes sense because it allows the *Guard* to reach younger readers they hope to ultimately convert to print readers. "We will, for instance, publish a late-breaking story online, not necessarily giving them the full story, but say, 'Pick up tomorrow's copy of the print *Register-Guard* for the full story.' And then, on the other hand, we may have a story in print that is a fairly in-depth story, but there may be a lot of additional information online. So we'll point back to the website. Hopefully we'll get people moving back and forth, and they'll be interested in both products."[18]

Downing said he doesn't think the Internet will mean the end of the print edition but acknowledges a great deal of opinions from "it doesn't hurt us at all" to "it's killing us." He said, "I go out there and I have people say to me, 'I don't need it. I get it on the Internet free.' That's one person lost. I figured out that it's about five hundred eighty dollars a year in terms of circulation and preprint revenue per subscriber, just based on our internal statistics. I guess the point being that anybody you lose is a bad deal. On the other hand, if the Internet evolves to the point that it is supplementing and helping circulation, I think that can be a great thing."[19] The *Guard* requires visitors to its website to register, a strategy used at many other newspapers. Online visits are increasing but cannot be counted until a likeness of the newspaper is available online in a PDF format. Registration numbers indicate that three-quarters of the people that are registered have nothing to do with the print version of the newspaper, Downing said. "A lot of them are new to the community; a lot of them are resident bloggers or people who are familiar with the net," including those from the University of Oregon. He expects the Internet could drive some readers to the newspaper, and if it does, then the *Guard* will have some opportunities.[20]

In 2006 the *Guard* raised its price. Sunday single copies went from $1.25 to $1.50, Tony said, because all costs are creeping up and they were a little underpriced in the market. It was the first time in a dozen years there had been an increase in the price of the Sunday paper. Single copy Monday through Saturday has remained at $0.50 for a dozen years or more.

One strategy Tony implemented in 2005 to enhance the business decisions the company makes and to improve its performance both short term and long term was to add the outside perspective of three independent, nonfamily members to the board. They are Mason Sizemore, retired COO of the Seattle Times Company; Kathy Bussman, a member of the Follett Book Publishing family in Chicago; and Dan Ambrose, who runs a sales-training company. The company has a twenty-four-member board of directors, and the new outside directors are a part of the smaller eleven-member executive committee or what Tony calls the "working board." He said he had championed the idea for some time and the family finally warmed up to the idea. Although it was a tough sell, ultimately he believes it was a good business decision. "My conviction and my belief—and I've done a lot of soul-searching about it—is we need to do this if we're going to be stronger moving forward," he said. Today the company stresses a heightened sense of accountability among department heads and himself. The influence of the outside directors has been helpful, he said. When the board sat down to approve the 2006 budget, "Lo and behold [the new members] said, 'Let's do some more work on that.' ... So I went back to the managers and we retooled it ... It's healthier than the budget we submitted" earlier. Tony said he believes the influence of the independent directors will help the newspaper grow out of today's tough times and be more profitable and successful in the long term.

In addition to changing the makeup of the board, Tony said one of his priorities is to look at long-range projections and future leadership of the company. Some family owned newspapers have no one in line to take over. But at the *Guard*, there are plenty of Bakers. In addition to Tony and Dave Baker, Edwin M. Baker is chairman of the board, Bridgett Baker Kincaid is over corporate public relations, and Richard Baker Jr. oversees information systems for the newspaper. The big question, however, is whether there is someone in the fourth generation who will be willing and ready to take control of the company when the time comes. Of course, another option is to find a nonfamily member who is just the right fit to run it.

As the shares of the company pass from the second to the third generation, there will be more decisions to be made. Some family members who are not involved in the day-to-day operations may be willing to sell their shares back to the company. To the next generation, Tony said, "If you'd like to be in for the long haul, that's fine, but that means there might be some financial sacrifice to be in for the long haul. If you're interested in doing other things, we certainly recognize that as a shareholder that's your right. But if you're interested [in working here], here are the steps you need to go through to realize that benefit." Given the interests of the fourth generation today, if he had to bet he would say that's a long shot "only because there aren't that many who have expressed an interest or demonstrated that this is a profession they want to go into. Now, we could be surprised."

The company has real estate holdings in addition to the newspaper. Tony said the company owns buildings in downtown Eugene and forty-seven acres of undeveloped industrial property. He said the company purchased twenty acres next to them in 1989, and it has quadrupled in value since then. "We really want the newspaper to stand on its own, but we're getting some pretty good cash flow off the real estate," he said.[21] The challenge, he said, is to remain independent. Emphatically vowing, "we're not for sale," Little said, "It's not a question of satisfying the stockholders who don't care whether they own McClatchy or Microsoft. If they're looking for a profitable investment, then they will follow the money. In our case, the profit motive isn't as strong as it is with a publicly owned company." It's important to remain profitable to support the needs of the company and to fulfill its obligations to the owners, he said, "but we also want to invest in the product, invest in the community. I guess the best word I could use to describe it would be we want to be sustainable."

He said the company is not vulnerable to a buyout. "In a sense there's a lot less risk for us and we can afford to run the newspaper the way we want to. I think that will better serve the readers and the advertisers and make us more viable in the long run." Little said he thinks newspapers in the largest markets are suffering the most because of high turnover and less commitment or sense of community. He said he is "cautiously optimistic" about the future and hopes the difficult times the *Guard* and the rest of the industry face ultimately will be regarded as growing pains. The industry may be mature and stalled, but he hopes it is repositioning itself. "As an independent newspaper, I'm optimistic that we'll be able to leverage our position in the marketplace and our financial position through diversification in order to continue to sustain the business and perhaps grow our presence in the community." In that sense he is optimistic, "But I'm not naïve about it either. I think it's going to take a lot of change and a lot of work."[22]

LaCamp said he's optimistic that the *Guard* will stay independently owned "for many years to come, and they [the owners] will produce the best quality product that they can possibly produce." He said he believes it will get more difficult, but there are still enough readers who want a printed product. "We really strive hard to produce a quality paper, and I think we do a pretty dog-gone good job. Some newspapers don't care."[23]

In August 2009, the *Guard* cut 16 full-time positions, leaving 305 employees. Tony Baker blamed "a lousy economy." The newspaper had eliminated the equivalent of 35 full-time positions in June. Citing a drop in advertising revenue, Chief Operating Office David Pero said the *Guard*'s decline "is consistent with what's happening throughout the newspaper industry. ... Compared to our peer group, we're in the middle of the pack."[24] The newspaper's largest reported circulation is 74,150, according to the Audit Bureau of Circulations.

Notes

1   Bob Welch, "R-G owners celebrate 75 years," *Register-Guard*, March 3, 2002.
2   Ibid.
3   Tony Baker (publisher, *Register-Guard*), interview with the author, March 23, 2006.
4   Ibid.
5   Fletcher Little (former vice president, *Register-Guard*), interview with the author, March 23, 2006.
6   Little, interview.
7   Tony Baker, interview.
8   Ibid.
9   Little, interview.
10 Dave Baker (managing editor, *Register-Guard*), interview with the author, March 23, 2006.
11 Ibid.
12 Jerry LaCamp (production manager, *Register-Guard*), interview with the author, March 23, 2006.
13 LaCamp, interview.
14 InsideBayArea.com, Newspapers In Education, "Glossary of Newspaper Terminology," http://education.insidebayarea.com/newsschool/terms.asp.
15 La Camp, interview.
16 Charles Downing (circulation director, *Register-Guard*), interview with the author, March 23, 2006.
17 Downing, interview.
18 Little, interview.
19 Downing, interview.
20 Downing.
21 Tony Baker, interview.
22 Little, interview.
23 LaCamp, interview.
24 Ilene Aleshire, "Newspaper cuts staff by nearly 6 percent of work force: The full- and part-time Register-Guard job cuts are intended to offset a continued drop in advertising," *Register-Guard*, Aug. 18, 2009, http://special.registerguard.com/csp/cms/sites/web/business/18805695-41/story.csp.

Concord Monitor

I n 2006, a year when newspaper companies across the nation were cutting staff and news hole in the face of soaring operating costs and declining revenues, Newspapers of New England (NNE) expanded. The company made its first acquisition in twenty years when it bought the *Daily Hampshire Gazette* in Northampton, Massachusetts. NNE, parent company of the *Concord Monitor*, was debt free until the acquisition, because of the successful operation of the company and its flagship newspaper in Concord. The company also owns a weekly, the *Monadnock Ledger*, in Peterborough, New Hampshire, and two other dailies, the *Valley News* in West Lebanon, New Hampshire, and the *Recorder* in Greenfield, Massachusetts. Geordie Wilson, who took over as *Monitor* publisher in 2005, is optimistic about the future of the company and newspapers—if they are privately owned. He makes a distinction between private and public ownership as a predictor of the kind of newspaper that will survive and thrive in the twenty-first century.[1] Acknowledging that there are "some terrible family owned newspapers," Wilson said the big predictor of success is a different operating philosophy. "Not that we're not interested in making money or doing well financially, but what we do with that money is different, and our time frame for reaping those kinds of financial rewards is different," he said.[2]

Publicly owned newspapers react aggressively and sometimes frantically to even the slightest budgetary fluctuations. At privately owned newspapers, the mindset is inwardly focused. "Quarterly or even annual swings are of concern, obviously, but they're not a concern in and of themselves," Wilson said. "If we're having bad quarters, bad years, they're a concern in that they may be pointing to operational problems or some other problems. On balance, we run on a much lower margin than the Gannettes of the world, and that's important. It allows us to invest more in the product, and that helps us."

The company adopted an institutional management style thirty years ago to operate more effectively, a move that changed the company culture. In the old days, Wilson said, if a piece of equipment was needed, a manager could go to his grandfather to get approval to buy it. Today life is different. "Since the seventies, we've made a real attempt to professionalize the corporate management of the company in terms of estate planning, bringing in outside directors, formalizing board processes, and formalizing capital expense procedures." Wilson said he tries to apply the kinds of analyses he learned while working at Microsoft and in business school. "When we're considering a project, we try to do a really careful job of looking at paybacks and net present values." Board approval may be required, but "we're trying to maintain a balance between the flexibility that you get from just sole owner/sole proprietor kind of decision making and some of the more considered judgments that you can get from a more corporate process." He describes the corporate culture as one of trying to move fast, trying to be relatively informal, but trying to be thoughtful—a sort of mid-ground between a sole proprietorship and a public company.

One important move was to appoint members to the board who were outside the family. Currently there are three: John Kuhnz, publisher of the *Valley News*, also owned by NNE; Tom Brown, former president of NNE and former publisher of the *Monitor*; and Byron Campbell, a veteran newspaper executive. Conscientious financial planning was another important step. When Wilson's grandfather died, the process began to preserve family ownership. In 2005, a seven-year structuring plan was completed that included setting up a family trust to prevent future generations from ever having to sell the newspapers.[3]

The Monitor Operation

The basic business model that newspapers have followed for years is using content to attract readers, using readers to attract advertisers, and using revenue to reinvest and improve content and quality, which they hope will attract more advertisers and, thus, more revenue. Wilson embraces that virtuous cycle and believes if that focus holds, it will drive the rest of the business. Consequently, good journalism and successful business are not in opposition. But there are external factors—especially today—that are uncontrollable and can affect the viability of the basic model. "Those are tough, but why not control the things you can control," he said. "You can control the quality of the product you put out, and that does have an impact on your readership, on the satisfaction of your advertisers, and the support of the community." The extremes are obvious. If an owner cuts news hole to cut expenses, the quality of the reporting diminishes and eventually readers will notice. The product will become less important to them, they will become less engaged, and they will not buy it as frequently. At the *Monitor*, "we do the best we can afford to," Wilson said. "We spend a much higher percentage of our revenue on the newsroom, and that's been a strategic decision going back forty years at least. We're going to do the best journalism we can. It's a statement of faith that's central to everything we do, that if we do the best newspaper we possibly can, the business side will ultimately take care of itself."

But doing good journalism is expensive. The basic journalistic truth—"do good journalism and the profits shall follow"—is less true today where the notion of a daily printed newspaper is under assault, Wilson said. Maintaining a comparatively large newsroom staff is not easy. It is a bold move to focus on high quality when newspapers are facing considerable structural industry change. "It may have been a slightly unusual decision to really focus on that and doing that kind of quality in a small daily newspaper out in New Hampshire," he said. "It's harder now, I think, than it was." But he thinks the basic business model is still sound "if we can get through the period of disruption."

Wilson, the fourth generation of his family to work in the business, was a reporter at the *Greeley Tribune* in Greeley, Colorado, and the *Seattle Times*. He was city editor at the *Monitor* in the mid-1990s and publisher of the *Monadnock Ledger* until 2003.[4] He made calculated decisions to go back to business school and to take a job at Microsoft and Starwave "because I do think that we have to understand these technologies in order to survive." In today's world of Internet publishing, there are different competitors and a faster pace of technological change. Fast forward even ten years and the world of newspapers will be different. "I don't know what we're going to look like," he said. "It's clear that electronic publishing, web publishing, and various other forms are increasingly changing the way people are choosing to consume at least parts of what we get out of a newspaper now." It is possible that newspapers could become a boutique medium. "We used to have 80 percent readership. Now we have 70 percent readership. Maybe we're going to have 40 percent readership, but it's going to be the elites, the business elites, the educated elites. That's not a terrible position to be in. Those are good people for advertisers," Wilson said. There may be fewer of them, but there is still value in reaching them. "The act of reading printed products is not going away. The daily newspaper habit, the kinds of news people are reading, the kind of newspaper products they want to pick up—that's changing." The tech-savvy publisher sees many opportunities, he said.

Newspapers today face organizational and structural challenges to getting into a position to be more entrepreneurial in launching products. "It now costs a lot of money to get into play," Wilson said. Societal changes also present opportunities. For example, today there are long lines at coffee shops every morning—something uncommon ten years ago. That development is a real opportunity for newspapers, but it is equally threatening because companies have to figure out how to respond. It may require taking on more expenses or being more nimble about how employees are used even in the newsroom.

Some newspapers are launching new products, like lifestyle magazines and car guides. But Wilson said newspapers need to be more flexible and quicker in figuring out where they need to go and look at a broader array of printed products as well as electronic ones. "We've got to bet on more horses going forward, but we have to be smart in knowing how to place those bets. Not just in picking the right horses, because nobody can pick all the right horses, but in being smart enough not to bet the house on every horse that we see that we like," he said.

The *Monitor* publishes several special sections, a combination of editorial, advertising, and both. But "we don't really do any significant publications that live outside the newspaper. Everything lives primarily as a special section within the newspaper." Wilson does not discount future consideration of outside products, however, like a lifestyle magazine, for instance.

Like most newspapers, the *Monitor*'s circulation is declining. Wilson expects a drop of better than 6 percent. But what is of more concern to the publisher is that "we are losing relevance as we are losing penetration." In general, advertising at the *Monitor* has been steady, but there are still challenges even though ad rates increase annually. One problem is that auto dealers across the country are now looking at what role newspaper advertising should play in their portfolio. But Wilson is more concerned about smaller advertisers. "The fact [is] that you could raise your basic open rate every year, and you leave behind more and more and more advertisers. The metric that I want to look at more carefully is the number of advertisers, number of ads, more than just average inch rate and revenue. There are 2,500–3,000 businesses in the Concord community, and we get 600–700 a month that are advertising with us. What about the other 2,300 advertisers? Why aren't they advertising with us?"

There are different ways to look at newsroom expenditures, Wilson said. The industry rule of thumb is to keep it at 11–12 percent of revenue. Another is to look at what you are getting in circulation revenue. "Is your circulation covering your news operation?" he said, quoting NNE President Tom Brown as calling that method "a gut check." Are people willing to pay for the editorial product? If you're not getting very much money in circulation and you're spending a great deal of money in editorial, maybe people aren't really willing to pay for what you're putting into it. You either try to get people to pay for that or think about not putting quite so much in. "That's a metric that we look at," he said. More traditional is the practice of looking at circulation revenue and if that covers the cost of basic production—printing and distribution of the newspaper. Those are the numbers corporations primarily look at, he said. "But I like Tom's, too, because that gets at a gut level. Are people willing to put down fifty cents on the counter to pick up your paper?" Are they supporting your editorial effort? A private, family owned newspaper can choose the model to follow even though some family newspapers take their numbers very seriously and strictly enforce them, especially those that own small newspaper chains. In the end Wilson said, "We keep in mind several yardsticks—Tom's newsroom cost-coverage measures, the circulation and production cost measure, and also the percent of revenue measure, except that we tend to aim not for 11–12 percent but more like 17.5–18 percent of revenues over time, and we try not to react abruptly to bring things into line."

The *Monitor*'s strategy to grow readership is through aggressive and more sophisticated marketing of the newspaper. Supporting a large staff of extraordinary editors and reporters, and implementing a continuous redesign cycle has also helped. The newspaper's focus on visual presentation has led the *Monitor* to win awards for design. "The paper is better now than it has been in years, so we're continuing to improve what we do," Wilson said. "We're having lots of discussions about the importance of visual editing, the importance of different content streams, the importance of incorporating the kinds of discussions that go on in our recently launched blog site, trying to bring that content into the paper, trying to flow things back and forth." Wilson believes the possibilities for engaging readers and gaining deeper reader involvement is virtually endless, and the *Monitor* has made a strong commitment to working smarter, improving content, and being more effective marketers.

Embracing Technology

Flexography printing technology has brought the company a marketable advantage in large part because of the bright colors it makes possible. "We're going to be the best printed newspaper in the country," Wilson said. Maximizing the value of the flexo printing press that was installed about sixteen years ago has become a highly successful strategy. Wilson said the company prints eighty-five different commercial client publications. "We are approaching twenty-four-hour-a-day production, so we are one of the few newspapers in the country to successfully develop a commercial printing business."

Instead of offset, which is based on oil and water, flexography is "potato print." Wilson described the process: "You have a kind of rubbery coating on a steel plate, and you apply ultraviolet light though film, which then conditions the rubbery surface so that when you put it through basically just hot water and soap-washing machines, it washes away, carves out the 'potato,' and leaves tiny little rubbery pixels. Then you put that plate on a plate cylinder, the plate cylinder runs across a sponge cylinder that stores ink, puts ink onto the little rubbery pixels, and then it goes onto the paper in an impression cylinder. It's potato printing the newspaper."

There are big advantages to flexo technology. It uses nonpolluting ink, there is no smearing, which affects the kind of paper that can be used, and it produces bright colors. Production-wise, a flexo press cuts down on staff. "The thing about a flexo press is, you turn it on, and as soon as you get your registration in, as soon as you line things up, which you can do pretty quickly, it runs unattended. You don't have to be there adjusting each machine. It just starts and goes." The speed is about the same as an offset press. The result is a press that runs all day, allowing the company to maximize production and cut expenses. "On Tuesdays and Wednesdays, we're doing commercial jobs from five in the morning to eleven at night, one after the other, and the day shift is two guys running that press," Wilson said.

It takes only two workers to run the press, and it is cost effective. Unlike offset, where an apprenticeship is required, flexo doesn't require extensive training and the expense of finding press operators. The *Monitor* likes to hire workers who have some printing background, but they are looking for people who are somewhat mechanical and can be trained to operate a press within six months.

There is no significant difference between the cost of a flexo press and the cost of an offset press. The real difference is that flexo has much less waste, so the *Monitor* has huge runs, and paper waste is not as great.

The problem with flexography, however, is that there is only one supplier of plates, which Wilson said may be the biggest hurdle for other newspapers to go flexo. About fifty newspapers use the technology. "But [when] we look at our numbers, our production costs are lower than comparable papers our size, and I know it's because of flexo," he said.

Wilson said embracing new technology is in keeping with his father's philosophy: If you can reduce the time, effort, and cost of putting ink on paper, you can do more in the newsroom. Wilson said he's a firm believer that good journalism will drive strong business. The *Monitor* was one of the earliest newspapers in the country to use computers in the newsroom. The justification in the past for bringing in new technologies has been the ability to shift staff from composing to editing. "You use your technology to pare down your expenses, not for the sake of paring down your production expenses, but for the sake of freeing up the opportunity to invest in your news product and make it better," he said.[5]

Brown, former president and CEO of Newspapers of New England, said the company has always been willing to take the long-term view on capital projects, pointing to the flexo press. Thinking long term for the company, with high-quality production and the environment, with water-based rather than petroleum-based inks, was easier because it is family owned. George W. Wilson, Geordie's father, was willing to take the risk, invest, and look long term in building a state-of-the-art building, said Brown, who has been with the company about twenty years. It would have been a harder decision in a public company. "To take the risk of investing in new unproven technology, and at the same time to make a hard analysis of return on investment that spending millions of dollars—in our case for a paper of twenty-two-thousand circulation—might not have passed the test in a lot of public companies," he said.[6] But by being willing to make that investment, now sixteen years later, it's paid off.

The ability to rationalize that kind of investment over a longer period of time without worrying about whether the stock is going up or down is another characteristic of a family owned company. Even though the family evaluates the company's stock periodically, owners are willing for it to be worth less one year than another if they believe that making a wise investment will pay off long term. "I think that helps preserve your newspaper franchise," Brown said. Being able to expand into the new commercial printing business not only helps rationalize the press and the building, but also directly helps reduce the cost of the news operation. Commercial printing represents about 20 percent of the company's revenue, he said.

Local autonomy and good management that understands that the company, even though it is family owned, must operate with financial discipline help explain the *Monitor*'s strength as a business. Brown said having independent members of the board and quarterly meetings—where the board discusses what makes a good newspaper and why the newspaper company is more than just a business—keeps everyone focused. "A successful business makes successful newspapers" that serve their communities. "We aren't just people hired for a few years looking for the next opportunity," Brown said. "They [the owners] are living this business, and it's their future."

Not unlike public companies, the *Monitor* keeps a strong eye on efficiency. Not every family owned newspaper has good management, but Brown believes a successful company starts with the quality of the ownership, be it public or private. At the *Monitor*, the owners know what they're doing and are highly competent. "I just can't say because now I'm in a company that doesn't have to worry about quarterly stock reports that it [financial performance] doesn't matter. It does matter," he said. "You have to make good cash flow. You have to pay attention to efficiencies. But if you do all those things, then you have the ability to ride it up and down a little bit because the economy goes up and down." Many public companies expect cash flow to grow 10–15 percent every year, he said. It's more important to try to achieve a steady 20 percent cash flow instead of 30, and to invest in the newsroom and technology. "Our industry suffers from people trying to get 30 and 40. You can do it for a while, but you can't do it forever and not have the product eroded," he said.

He said as president and CEO it is his job to run the company as a solid business. If you want to keep a company private and successful, have money to invest, buy new presses and run great newsrooms, then you have to bring some business discipline, he said. "I think some family newspapers in the past have probably suffered and even been sold out for that reason, because they weren't run in that manner. But beyond that, I think the big difference is the focus. It's long term and they really seriously have the ability to take a longer view, not only from the business perspective but from a community and from a journalistic perspective."

Additionally there can be more community loyalty and stronger emotional feelings toward the family owners, he said. In turn, the owners can feel closer to their community. "Newspapers of New England—and the *Concord Monitor*—rises and falls on the success of its community," Brown said. Newspapers are tied to the community. "We care about our community. And if the community doesn't succeed, neither do we." He said at public companies often there is churning of publishers and editors, especially in small and mid-size cities. While there is value in bringing in new people with new ideas, many publishers of publicly owned companies are really focused on where they are going next. It's a different mindset from planning to spend your life in a community, he said. Brown said he thinks the community knows that the owners are in Concord for the long term and not just the newest public company publisher to come to town to make a name for himself.

About twenty years ago, NNE executives helped start the PAGE Cooperative Board to help independent privately owned newspapers buy newsprint and other supplies in a cost-effective way. In addition to collaborating on cost savings, one advantage of PAGE is the opportunity to meet a few times a year with other newspaper owners and publishers. "They care greatly about their newspapers, and they all make different decisions," Brown said. But they share a common long-term commitment to their community and believe that the newspaper is more than just a business.

Investing in the News

The *Monitor* was voted by the *Columbia Journalism Review* in 1999 and *Time* magazine in its September 29, 1997 issue as one of the best newspapers in America. Brown said the family spends 20–25 percent more than average on news. The newsroom has about forty-five full-time employees, about twice the national average for a newspaper of twenty-two-thousand circulation. The *Monitor*'s news hole is five to six pages larger than average. "So far we've been able to run a daily newspaper with four sections with color on every page. [We have] the kind of quality you would expect from maybe a paper of forty-thousand circulation, not twenty-two thousand," Brown said. "We have a deep commitment to journalism and quality news." Spending money makes a difference.[7]

The news hole has grown tighter though, choices former Editor Mike Pride said are manageable with taller ad stacks. "It's really a matter of going with all sixes instead of six, eight, six, eight," he said, referring to number of pages in sections. "If we can accommodate that, we do. There is some loss of news hole, but it's not great."[8]

Overall the size of the staff at the newspaper is about 165 people, with 140 FTEs, Wilson said. Even in tough times, those numbers have remained fairly stable. Laying off staff has never been a strategy at the *Monitor*. "We didn't have to do any layoffs in the last recession" in the early 1990s, he said, calling that economic downturn cataclysmic in New Hampshire. "I don't know that we've ever done layoffs." However the owners are careful about filling positions. There have been times when positions "went dark" or were left unfilled. But that strategy might not be as hard in Concord as in other places. The *Monitor* has a reputation as a top-notch newspaper but also as a training ground for young reporters who spend a few years, take advantage of covering national politics during the New Hampshire primary, then move on to much bigger newspapers. They are also motivated to move on by higher salaries in bigger cities. That means there is churn in the newsroom, which helps the owners manage staff size through attrition.[9]

Pride, who retired from the *Monitor* in 2008, said in the thirty years he's been at the *Monitor*, there have never been wholesale staff cuts. "I've been the managing editor or the editor through three recessions, and we have never laid anybody off," he said.[10] "We've allowed positions to go dark; we've cut corners; we've cut overtime; we've done what managers have to do in getting the paper through crises like that. But we're not tied to a quarter-to-quarter mentality." He said there is a sense in the company that there will be good times and bad times, and managers have to be able to manage in both environments. There is no sense that if percentages or numerical goals are unmet that drastic actions will have to be taken. "If you've got a commitment to community journalism, it's something that will have the strength to roll through good times and bad," he said.

Pride said he has known Geordie Wilson since he was fourteen years old and has worked for two other publishers, Wilson's father and Brown, who served between George and Geordie. It's the continuity of the family ownership that makes the company successful. One important advantage is the way the family made the decision to pass the newspaper on to the next generation and to train them not only in the values of journalism but also in the importance of newspapers in their community. Pride sees that as key to the company's strength.

Speedy Decisions

Being able to act quickly especially during today's dynamic environment sets the *Monitor* apart from large newspaper chains, Pride said. "We're always evaluating the newspaper on the basis of its content and whether it matches what we think readers want." The owners aren't afraid to experiment. In another environment, there would be endless meetings, planning, and discussions about what direction the newspaper will take. "In our case, I think we just decide to go, and we go. It's an age where, because of the changing media environment, you really need to be able to react very quickly to things. I think we have a great advantage in the ability to do that here."[11]

Buying the *Daily Hampshire Gazette* was an example of seizing an opportunity when the time was right. Brown said the decision to buy the newspaper started while dining with former *Gazette* Publisher Peter DeRose and another NNE publisher to discuss collaborating on some initiatives because of the proximity of the Greenfield paper. "In fact, it didn't even start with talk about buying Pete's paper," he said. The families had known each other for years. So, when the conversation turned to the future of the *Gazette* and DeRose's attempts to find good owners, Brown and the NNE board saw a chance to expand the company and preserve family ownership in Northampton. "We were certainly able to make a decision fast," he said.[12]

The importance of timing is a mindset that filters down to news coverage decisions. Today, managers are developing the newspaper's website, soliciting comment and content from readers, and blogging—all as part of the *Monitor*'s continuous reevaluation of the way it provides information. New beats are created periodically as the newspaper evolves, and the managers stay flexible within the high standards of quality they have set for themselves. One opportunity came during the devastating New England floods of May 2006. The web allowed the newsroom to produce an interactive map and to publish photos, shot both by *Monitor* photographers and by readers. "We had people in the community sending us snapshots that we tied to the map," Pride said. "So you could look in your own neighborhood and you'd see photographs that people had taken there. ... We had tremendous response, and we had so many readers write letters saying, 'We used that, and we thank you for doing it.' It was a fantastic public service." Today the *Monitor* is doing more timely journalism on the web using the creativity and imagination of a tech savvy young staff to make it work. Streaming audio and video are part of that development.

So far the *Monitor* has resisted putting ads on the front page of the newspaper. "We have an open A1; we have an open A2; we have open section fronts," Pride said, as well as an open editorial page. The priority is keeping the newspaper well organized for readers. "I think we probably as a newsroom have more control over that than most places," he said.

The bottom line, Pride said, is that journalism is a service, and serving the community comes first to the newspaper's owners. The new generation will face tremendous challenges, but he expects them to take advantage of those to find new ways to do their jobs. "You can't beat a macroeconomic trend, but within your own market, I think you can be really prepared to take advantage of opportunities and create opportunities. I think we're doing that." He said he expects the media to continue to change the way information is presented but "that notion that we're here to serve the community and to be a consistent, reliable source of information, put every dollar and every good idea that we can into that—I just don't think that's going to change, and I think that's the first priority for this family." There are plenty of families who own newspapers who are not motivated in the same way as the *Monitor* owners. "They have a lot of power, and they have a lot of ways in which they can exercise that power. Ours just happen to have, to me, the right values," he said.[13]

For former Managing Editor Felice Belman, the *Monitor* operating model was enough to bring her back to Concord after a stint at the *Washington Post*. She worked at the *Monitor* at age twenty-two right out of college, then found herself willing to take a 50 percent pay cut to leave the *Post* to become part of a team of senior editors in Concord who recognize that they are in a special place. "That's a big decision, but it was worth it because it's just such a pleasure to come to work most days," she said.[14]

In early 2006 when an opportunity arose to send a reporter to El Salvador with the National Guard, Belman got the resources she needed to make the story happen. That same year—a particularly challenging one economically—the newsroom sent a reporter to spring training with the Red Sox and to Columbus, Ohio, for an Episcopal Church gathering because the Episcopal bishop of New Hampshire was at the center of a gay rights controversy. Resources are not unlimited, Belman said, but "we're able to do a lot of stuff within confines. They [the owners] really push excellence." Newsroom staffing levels have remained the same through challenging times.

Belman credits owners who are journalists first for the strong focus on a quality newsroom. Wilson is willing to take risks, think big, move quickly, and try new things, she said. "He's fun to work for." The family is also low-key and doesn't push pet projects or coverage of their special interests. "We're blessed with owners who don't meddle in the newsroom and are helpful."

She said the focus of the newsroom is on local coverage, but today "it behooves us not to think of ourselves as paper producers so much as news producers." Nowhere else but the *Monitor* will provide readers with all the news about Concord. "You're not going to get it out of television, or if you subscribe to the [Boston] *Globe* or the *New York Times*. So we're providing a service that nobody else is. I think it's valuable in a way that we're giving people what they can't get anywhere else," she said.[15]

The Team Approach

Ann-Marie Forrester, retail advertising director, and Deborah Sanborn, clas-sified/national advertising director, say they look for opportunities to save money and work efficiently. They have both made commonsense cuts includ-ing doing away with a proofreader, Forrester said, because that should be the responsibility of the sales rep, and an ad tracker who made sure the ads were OK'd at the end of the night. The graphic designers can do that, she said. They decided to hold off on hiring an ad coordinator "not because we were told to, [but] because we can see how maybe we can run a little more efficiently by not having that person."[16] Their incentive? To save the company money, For-rester said. "We're not getting any perks for that at all," Sanborn said. "We do everything to help the company."[17]

Forrester said she and Sanborn are extremely frugal and have full access to the budgets. "We know how much money comes in; therefore, we can limit our spending. We take care of our staff. That comes first in our eyes." They hold onto equipment and don't spend frivolously. "We look out for the welfare of the newspaper." She said they think about the big picture, not just advertising, but online, the newsroom, circulation, everything that affects them because that will help make their paper better. Ultimately, she said, "NNE would take care of us if we took care of them, and they definitely do. They appreciate you."[18]

David Hanks, former director of circulation, said among the company's strengths are the owners' focus on trying new techniques to build circulation. Being able to pick up the phone and access the president or publisher when problems arise, then having the ability to take action quickly when needed is the philosophy of the company.

Hanks said a new initiative in the works is using credit cards in newspaper vending machines. Changing consumer purchasing behavior led to the idea. "I don't carry change. I don't carry cash, but I do carry my debit card," Hanks said. The *Monitor* has found a vendor who has developed a mechanism that has security in place. It accepts Visa or MasterCard and is a simple process whereby the consumer slides a card into the mechanism that reads it and veri-fies the card, then allows the door to open. From there, collection employees using an audit card access the transactions from the newspaper boxes and come back to the *Monitor* for further processing. Security-wise, Hanks doesn't believe there is any more risk using credit card newspaper boxes than a typical ATM. "My gut feeling is that if there's somebody who wants access to credit cards, your newspaper box is probably not going to be the best avenue." Some boxes have thirty papers, others far fewer, he said. Theft is avoided because the boxes are already chained down with heavy cement boxes in the bottom.

Thinking world-class customer service has led the *Monitor* to offer delivery per the subscriber's request. "We'll put it at the door; we'll put it between the doors," Hanks said. "We have some subscribers who have health issues, and the independent contractors understand that some people can't bend over because of a medical condition and that we're going to put it up on that table for them." It's simply going the extra mile for the subscribers "because we believe inherently that if we treat them well, they're going to continue to treat us well. And so far, so good," he said.

The *Monitor* has followed the industry trend of moving from youth to adult carriers, although youth are sought to fill some routes. It's an opportunity to provide jobs for youth, who can sign on at fourteen. "They get to the age that they can deliver, and they keep it through high school," Hanks said. Retention rate for both carriers and drivers is 40–50 percent. "We have fifty-eight motor routes and approximately ninety-six foot routes. Of those foot routes, we have about thirty youth carriers, and the rest are adults," he said.

About 99.8 percent of the *Monitor*'s subscriptions are prepaid, with the majority of them office pay. "We send them a bill upon renewal," Hanks said. "We have our standard cycles that most newspapers have, and we get a good return on that." An easy-pay system using automatic bank drafts was launched about three years ago and has been successful. "When you're on easy pay, people don't pick up the phone to say, 'I no longer want it.' It's kind of like your gym membership that even if you don't go, you still pay for it." Online bill paying is also an option. The *Monitor* promotes renewing and paying online through its website.

Like all newspapers, the *Monitor* has been forced to use creative strategies to bring in new sales, especially in light of Do-Not-Call (DNC) lists. Telemarketing laws have really hurt newspapers, Hanks said. "It was not uncommon prior to the DNC list being established that we could top fifty, sixty, seventy orders a week. To get twenty orders a week now is like pulling teeth," he said. So, the company is using kiosks in front of stores, including Walmart. Sales staff also work fairs and special events, do door-to-door sales, and use direct mail. A program was launched about three years ago with local hotels to sell them the newspaper at a reduced rate if they would agree to deliver that paper to the door of guests' rooms. The newspaper has also undertaken an initiative to do an in-depth study of the demographics of the market "to get the scope of what our reader looks like in different geographic areas," Hanks said. It is all in the interest of building readership.[19]

Unlike most public companies, journalistic imperatives drive the company's future. Focusing on local news—specifically being "intelligently local" or "thoughtfully local"—is the *Monitor*'s strategy. Wilson said the goal is to provide the kind of news that readers need. That doesn't mean covering every planning-board meeting, for example. It does mean doing bigger stories that result from routine meetings. Ultimately "it's the stories of broader interest, played well, played attractively, making connections that are going to distinguish us" into providing the kinds of news our readers can't get anywhere else, he said. "Good journalism drives readers" and business.[20]

Pride retired from the *Monitor* in 2008, and Belman was named editor. Brown retired from his post with NNE in 2009.

Notes

1   Geordie Wilson (publisher, *Concord Monitor*), interview with the author, May 26, 2006.
2   Wilson, interview.
3   Wilson.
4   Wilson.
5   Wilson.
6   Tom Brown (former president and CEO, Newspapers of New England), interview with the author, May 26, 2006.
7   Brown, interview.
8   Mike Pride (former editor, *Concord Monitor*), interview with the author, May 26, 2006.
9   Wilson, interview.
10 Pride, interview.
11 Pride.
12 Brown, interview.
13 Pride, interview.
14 Felice Belman (former managing editor, *Concord Monitor*), interview with the author, May 26, 2006.
15 Belman, interview.
16 Ann-Marie Forrester (retail advertising director, *Concord Monitor*), interview with the author, May 26, 2006.
17 Deborah Sanborn (classified/national advertising director, *Concord Monitor*), interview with the author, May 26, 2006.
18 Forrester, interview.
19 David Hanks (former director of circulation, *Concord Monitor*), interview with the author, May 26, 2006.
20 Wilson, interview.

8

Daily Hampshire Gazette

After thirty-six years at the helm of the *Daily Hampshire Gazette* in Northampton, Massachusetts, Peter DeRose finally took a step that is inevitable at many family owned newspapers. He sold the paper to Newspapers of New England (NNE), owners of the *Concord Monitor*, effective January 1, 2006.

It may have been a tough decision, but he had little choice. The simple fact is there was no succession plan for the newspaper's future. DeRose has no children, and his brother, Charles, copublisher of the *Gazette* until he retired seven years earlier, has children who were not interested in running a newspaper. "We had never planned for succession," DeRose said.[1] "We had not looked at a DeRose dynasty. Some people, it's important to them, but our philosophy has always been the next generation should do what they do best and what they like."

So, DeRose took the most attractive route. He found a like-minded newspaper family he had known for thirty years and turned over his ownership. But he did not walk away immediately. DeRose continued as publisher for a year during the transition. On January 1, 2007, Aaron Julien, who had been general manager of the *Gazette* since the sale, succeeded him. Jim Foudy became publisher in 2009 when Julien was named president of NNE. Acknowledging that he could have sold to a number of other companies, including publicly traded ones, DeRose is happy with the sale. "We could've flogged it around and had an auction and probably gotten considerably more money, but it would've been a lot of work, it would have been a lot of effort, and there was always a chance that people wouldn't have been interested. So I think we did fairly well as to the value of the paper." He hopes NNE will preserve the *Gazette*'s family ownership tradition.[2]

The *Gazette*, the longest continually published newspaper in Massachusetts, traces its history back 225 years to the end of the Revolutionary War. Harriet

Williams DeRose, a Smith College graduate who had been business manager at the *Gazette*, bought the newspaper in 1929. In 1960 her son, Charles N. DeRose, became publisher when she died. His two sons, Peter and Charles, took over as copublishers in 1970.

In addition to the *Gazette*, the DeRoses sold the weekly *Amherst Bulletin* and *Many Hands*, an alternative medical publication, to NNE, which owns the *Concord Monitor* in Concord, New Hampshire; the *Recorder* in Greenfield, Massachusetts; the *Valley News* in West Lebanon, New Hampshire; and the weekly *Monadnock Ledger*, in Peterborough, New Hampshire.[3]

Attractive Market

Julien, the previous publisher of the *Gazette* and a member of the NNE family, said Northampton was an attractive market for the company's expansion because it is tremendously vibrant. There are five colleges and universities in the area and people who are opinionated, have strong views on all sides of issues, and care deeply about their community. He met with local advertisers and others to assure them that they are not going to lose their newspaper to outsider owners. The strong ties between the Wilson and Dwight families at NNE and the DeRoses have led readers to see the new owners as having strong local connections. "The family had a long history in this valley," Julien said. "We have a lot of family members here, and people grew up here. There is some connection with the past, and that was very important to people in the community. ... I don't think we're perceived as outsiders." The DeRose family and the Dwight family have been business partners in the past, through joint ownership of television and radio stations.

Keeping writers and editors in place is a deliberate strategy to reassure *Gazette* readers. The same people who were producing the newspaper before January 1, 2006, are the same people who are producing it today under the NNE ownership. "Everything has stayed the same," Julien said. The transition was seamless. Most important in a newspaper acquisition is the way the ownership change takes place and that a local voice is retained. The new owners recognize that the *Gazette* is a tremendously important part of the community," he said. "There is no other unifying point in Hampshire County for all the voices that have to be heard on various issues, and this is the place that people look to." A community must have a place where they can learn about what is going on. Likewise, they need someone to run the paper who cares about the community enough to invest in reporters, spend the time needed to get their reporting right, and is honest and clear about the events that take place.

Julien said NNE can bring valuable assets to the table. Among them are the expertise and support that comes with owning more than one newspaper. But the biggest contribution is more capital and resources because as a larger company "we have a greater ability to make investments in the paper." Family ownership allows a company to have a longer horizon for the needs of the business than those owned by publicly traded corporations. Newspapers require a tremendous amount of capital reinvestment to keep them going, especially today with rising operation costs, emerging technologies, and increased pressure from competition.

The reinvestment required for a newspaper to remain relevant to readers also takes a great deal of money. NNE is more willing to reinvest money in the company as an independent newspaper owner. "You don't have to provide a certain dividend to shareholders that you would have to [with a publicly traded company]. And that enables you to roll more of your money back to the papers," Julien said. Because NNE does not have to worry about public stock appreciation, the company is not grasping at short-term actions to boost profitability. "We're just plowing a huge amount of money back into these papers. And you can't do that if you're a public company." Ultimately the aim of the company is not to meet strict financial goals. "Profit is important, but profit for us is important as a way to make the paper stronger and to better serve the readers."

Nevertheless, Julien stressed that NNE is serious about setting budgets and expects its newspapers to meet their budgetary goals. "It's not that you have to make that budget for the purposes of making Wall Street happy. It's because we know we need the money for lots of things that we're going to be doing ... whether it's buildings or buying presses." The NNE board is made up mostly of family members who he said are well-informed about the newspaper operations and able to act quickly if decisions need to be made. A high priority of the board members is to make sure each newspaper is an autonomous voice in the community.

Channeling substantial funds to Northampton has not caused resentment in Concord, where the *Monitor* is NNE's premiere property, Julien said. In fact, many employees there thought it was about time the company acquired another newspaper. One reason for that sentiment is that NNE is a good company, "and people have been watching good papers go to bad owners," he said. It is important for a company to be diversified. NNE is not diversified across product lines because they own only newspapers, but being diversified geographically is strategic for the company as a whole. "What we gain is a more diversified stream of income from more locations, so any particular problem in any one location is softened," he said. The acquisition also may send a message to *Monitor* staff that the company is financially strong and able to expand even in softer economic times. Employees at the *Monitor* see what they do "as having a greater effect, perhaps, that the company is able to go out and save newspapers from turning into money machines."[4]

DeRose said the *Gazette*'s location made it especially attractive. "You couldn't invent a better place to publish a newspaper," he said.[5] The valley is populated with educated people, five colleges within their circulation area, and many families that are multiple newspaper readers. People choose the area as a prime relocation target because of its slower pace compared to other hectic New England cities. The local economy is education based, so it remains fairly stable. "We have lost virtually all of our manufacturing business, which was the original economy of New England. The valley was an area where water power was the main attraction. All of those mills now have turned into either housing or artist galleries or maybe, in a few lucky places, Internet businesses." The population is educated, young, concerned, passionate, and more activist than most. "So we have it all," DeRose said.

Circulation is divided among four areas, Jim Foudy, the former editor and current publisher, explains: the city of Northampton; the town of Amherst, where the University of Massachusetts is located; the city of Easthampton, a very different community from Northampton; and the hill towns or rural areas, mostly to the north and west.[6]

Despite predictions that the future is dim for newspapers, *Gazette* Advertising Director Mark Elliott said they are still highly desirable commodities. "You never see a newspaper that's for sale go unsold for very long." Ultimately, he believes that a newspaper that is firmly connected to its community will make more money than one that is not. The *Gazette* is in a strong position because "we have a good franchise here. The product is really good, the community is tied in with it, we have a good local advertising base, we have a pretty good big box base, we're in a good location," and the economy is fairly steady, Elliott said.[7]

Controller Priscilla Flynn said she thinks DeRose could have made a lucrative deal with several corporations when he decided to sell, but it made sense for him to choose NNE even though he might have earned a higher return on this investment elsewhere. But, she said, "I do not think that Peter would have sold to certain corporations because he cares too much about his newspaper, and he wouldn't want to see a new owner come in and immediately start cutting staff, cutting news hole, changing our focus, which is local news. And that would've happened with some of the national newspaper corporations."[8]

Role In the Community

Had he sold to another company, DeRose said it would have been unlikely he would have stayed on as publisher during the transition. But at sixty-six he said he could retire and "not feel bad about it." DeRose has changed directions more than once in his life. He started as a physicist, went into engineering, and then into newspapers. He took the position of newspaper publisher very seriously, seeing himself as having two roles: one as a coach to the people who work with him, hiring the best and helping them do their jobs in the best way they can "and in the way that's necessary to run a paper." But a publisher is also a "major contact between the paper and the community," DeRose said. Through those contacts, a publisher gets a feeling of what the community pulse is and can "make decisions for the good of both the paper and the community."

DeRose said his strategy was to get out as much as possible and to meet as many people as he could—but not by flaunting his position. "I would just say, 'I work at the paper, and I'm interested in helping the paper help you.' " A publisher's job is to ask questions and to develop a rapport with readers that leads to dynamic discussions. "I publish my phone number and always have," DeRose said, "and people call me. We have interesting—sometimes not fun—but interesting discussions." A long-term publisher can be tremendously valuable to a newspaper, but he can also get too close to a community, become a booster, and be reluctant to do the tough stories that are critical to the community, DeRose said.

The *Gazette*'s mission over the years has been to serve the people of the Central Pioneer Valley, Hampshire County, Northampton, Amherst, Easthampton, and surrounding communities with the news and advertising they need in their daily lives. The paper serves the businesses in the same area by giving them access to that audience. "If we can do that, we're doing our job," DeRose said. But the higher calling for a newspaper is to serve as an information medium in a free and vibrant democracy. "And while we've got to serve our commercial end in order to survive, we've got to serve that other end in order for our democracy to survive." To DeRose, the company is not in the newspaper business but in the news business. "If we say newspapers, period, we run the risk of being buggy-whip manufacturers." The audience today "is the world we live in, and we have to make sure that those people are served. If they're not, we'll become extinct," he said.

DeRose is not sure the community cares whether the newspaper is locally owned and said newspapers overvalue themselves when they think the community does care. "What the community wants is a newspaper that meets its needs," he said. People want what works for them, and if a newspaper is more responsive to the needs of the community because the owners are local and their business policies are local, "that's a plus," he said.

Unlike some other media companies, the *Gazette* under the DeRose ownership did not expand into other industries. They bought a radio station but later sold it "because it was a distraction." In retrospect, DeRose said he doubts that was the right decision, but at the time it seemed to be. "I guess we've always felt that it made more sense to do one thing well than to do a lot of things and maybe not do some of them so well."[9]

Foudy said one big advantage of family ownership at a newspaper is the understanding the owners have of the readers and the market primarily because "the family members live here, they're local, they shop here, they deal with folks here." When changes are proposed, they always ask, does this make sense for their readership? Because family owned newspapers often have a truer sense of their readership, they can tailor the newspaper to the readers' needs. They can also produce lousy newspapers, if they are so entrenched in the community that they cannot see the bigger picture or their view of the readership is only the people they socialize with at the country club.[10]

Flynn said she thinks readers do care if the newspaper is family owned, because there is a perception that the family belongs to the community and what they write about is important to the community. Large corporate-owned newspapers are perceived as writing about what corporate tells them. If a newspaper is owned by a family, most of the time they have a common goal "and that is not necessarily to make as much money as possible," Flynn said. Advertisers care, too, because what they pay for in advertising stays in the community rather than "being funneled off to New York, Chicago, or other far reaches of the United States."

Flynn, who has worked for both publicly owned and family owned newspapers, said being owned by a national corporation can be valuable during crunch times because of greater resources and distant bosses. Local owners/ publishers take it very hard when they have to lay off employees and will try everything they can before taking that step. "For the [independent] publishers I've worked for, the owners of newspapers, making a certain percentage of profit every single year is not the most important thing. It's publishing the paper, and it's keeping their family together. And they consider the people who work for them as part of their family," she said. About 144 full-time and part-time employees work at the *Gazette*, and the largest department is editorial because of the strong focus on local news.[11]

Elliott, who also has worked for both publicly owned and family owned newspapers, said the reason the *Gazette* is so strong in Hampshire County has more to do with the ownership than it does with the fact that it is a newspaper. "Pete and his family have been very generous with the community," donating advertising space and taking an active role, he said. "I think people want to do business with people who are part of the community." Advertisers like for a newspaper to support the community and the things they do, and sponsorships of events or donations by the owners enhance their relationship with advertisers. A strong local focus is important, too. Local big box stores are big newspaper supporters, and "the viability of a local newspaper to them is great because it's a very inexpensive way for them to advertise twenty pages of product. So they like having strong newspapers in their communities."

Having more staff input and long-term thinking in decision making sets a family owned newspaper apart. In the corporate world, Elliott said, "you absolutely live by the month. It doesn't matter what next month is. It's just whatever the goal and number is [today] and what you can do to get there." At the *Gazette*, business may be bad this month or next month, but there is confidence in the system and that times will get better.

That kind of company culture leads to lower staff turnover than is typical in advertising departments at large corporate-owned newspapers. "We have very professional salespeople, and that's something that you tend not to find at chain-owned newspapers our size," Elliott said. The sales staff stays on— some as long as twenty to thirty years—because of the commissions they earn and the family work environment. That longevity, in turn, leads to stronger relationships with advertisers. "They [employees] are loyal to the paper, which is another thing you don't find in chain newspapers. There is a real loyalty because they are real people and a real family is behind it. And that loyalty is returned."

For Elliott, his experience at the *Gazette* has been working "for someone I also really like and respect and admire. When you work for a large chain, you always feel that I could get up and leave here today and be OK, and I have no emotional ties to it. [Employees] in the corporate part operate the same way. It's not that it's good or it's bad. It's just the way it is. It's definitely different [at the *Gazette*]," he said.[12]

Through the years, Foudy said he has weathered up-and-down economic cycles because he was able to look the owners in the eye across the table and say, "We're struggling here, and we're going to need some leeway this year; we're going to need a little flexibility in the budget." That flexibility often is not possible at big chains. At the *Gazette*, he has been confident the owners were not going to let the newspaper go bankrupt, and they are flexible in tight budget years. "They're willing to take a little less profit, or they're willing to do things a little differently to make it work. That, to me, is the enormous advantage that family owned papers have," he said.[13]

Flynn said the tighter controls NNE has instituted make departments more accountable and smarter with their budgets. With DeRose at the helm, managers could say, "We didn't make budget this month, but we've got plans in the future, and it's going to be OK," and DeRose would say, "That's OK." Today, she said, "we're discovering that ... we really need to make the budget." More synergies and greater buying power that come with the *Gazette* being part of a small group will offer more opportunities to save money, another advantage of the sale to NNE. "Family owned newspapers might have to work a bit smarter in the future, but I think they have a better chance of surviving," she said. She cites Knight Ridder as an example. They were a huge conglomerate, and that was picked apart. They almost went backward, she said. Being forced by share-holders to sell properties is less likely at family owned newspapers because, as independents, they have the power to make a conscious decision to accept less profit for the good of the paper and the good of the community.[14]

Foudy said NNE has a similar mindset and understands what the *Gazette* does because of the contact the two newspapers have had in the past and because they also are a family operation. He calls the NNE owners "straight shooters" and said they challenged *Gazette* managers to reevaluate the *Gazette*'s operations, to be more aggressive about decision making, and to think harder about their mission and how they execute it. Complacency is one of the disadvantages of family ownership. A family gets comfortable with their profit level and how their employees are compensated, and life goes on year to year. That is not the best scenario for growing the business, Foudy said. "Although Peter and his brother, Charlie, when he was involved, have been good publish-ers and thoughtful publishers, I think NNE is bringing thoughtful people who care about the community, but also a board that is going to be pushing us a little harder to ask some questions and live up a little better to our potential."

The *Gazette* sale came as a surprise to Foudy, but he is happy with the decision. Other companies had been knocking on the door, but NNE is a com-pany with a history of treating their employees well, he said. "These are good journalists who care about the newspaper business. They made a promise to us that there wouldn't be any staff cuts, and there haven't been." The NNE owners also promised they would look aggressively at the operation and seek ways to improve it.

Foudy is quick to point out that family ownership does not guarantee qual-ity journalism. That takes a strong commitment to the newspaper's mission and the willingness to devote resources to that end. He defines quality as a newspaper that covers the community well, gives readers enterprise stories, gets behind the news, and delivers a strong product. It is labor intensive, plain and simple. "While you can automate the hell out of the production end, you cannot automate the news gathering," he said, and "quality is necessary for survival."[15] The DeRoses insisted on maintaining a strong reporting staff. NNE is a company equally concerned about quality journalism and maintaining high editorial staffing levels in defiance of national ratios of staff per thousand circulation, Foudy said.

Julien agreed. Quality should be priority number one at a newspaper. "My belief is that content drives everything. Circulation is driven by content. Circu-lation is driven by the newsroom. If people don't want it, they're not going to pick it up," he said.[16] Julien attributed the decline in circulation at newspapers nationwide in part to their lower relevance to readers. If it is not relevant, people should not buy it, he said.

The focus on local coverage is reflected in the heavy staffing levels at the *Gazette*, which, DeRose said, has about 50 percent more staff than comparably sized chain newspapers. "That's really our advantage because we do that amount of local coverage, which our competition and other papers in larger chains just can't afford to do."[17]

The *Gazette* has about fifty full-time newsroom employees, a number that has remained fairly stable over the years. The DeRoses were reluctant to compromise the newsroom and lay people off during tough times. They took that approach to cost cutting only as a last resort after saving positions through attrition or consolidation. In 1991 about ten employees were lost, and a couple were let go in 2000–2001. News hole has been shrinking because run-of-paper advertising has been shrinking. But, Foudy said, the *Gazette* has maintained about a 50:50 ratio of news to ads. The size of the paper is smaller. "When I came here, on a Thursday we'd have a sixty-four-page paper, and I think we've probably got thirty-six to forty now," he said. The average number of pages on a given weekday was forty-two about twenty years ago and is thirty-eight today. The *Gazette* moved to a fifty-inch web in the early 1990s following the national trend.

The *Gazette* solved the problem of no Sunday newspaper by partnering with the *Boston Globe* to deliver the Sunday *Globe* to *Gazette* readers. About 1,500–1,800 *Gazette* subscribers take the *Globe* on Sunday for eighty-eight cents. "It's a good deal," Foudy said. But starting a Sunday newspaper at the *Gazette*, perhaps in partnership with their sister paper in Greenfield, is a possibility. Reiterating that strong local coverage is the *Gazette*'s franchise and ultimately what readers want most, Foudy said, "If we can take the Sunday product and deliver the local news and kind of big picture regional stuff, what's happening beyond our boundaries in western Massachusetts and put stories in context, then we'll do fine."

One of the mistakes newsrooms make is thinking that because they are the local paper, simply getting it out there and on the newsstands will persuade people to buy it, Foudy said. There may be some reader loyalty to the local paper, but in the end they are buying a product, "and if you can deliver what they want, then they'll be loyal to you."

Breaking news on the website is already part of the daily operation, but Foudy expects that to expand. Staff-produced blogs are generating more traffic to the website. He said the challenge for the newsroom is to give readers more, either in sidebars or online, to make the print product tighter and brighter, and to direct readers where to go if they want more information on a subject.[18]

Julien agreed that improving the online operation is important at the *Gazette*. One of the biggest issues for newspapers is how to meet readers' needs, and owners should recognize that the Internet is a tool they can now use to help them reach their goals. Readers can go to the Internet and get news quickly, but one of the services newspapers offer is the ability to sort through the news and provide a thoughtful, organized analysis of the day's events—local and around the world. The Internet doesn't do that, Julien said. "People are going to get what they want whether you provide it or not. Someone will provide it." Newspapers' websites can be that fast and constantly updated news source for people throughout the day more effectively than television and radio. "So that's something that's worth a lot of investment in money and time and thought, and that's one thing that we're working on here."[19]

The newsroom is open to news tips from other departments at the newspaper because the publisher, ad reps, circulation employees, and others travel in different circles from the journalists. "The newsroom can be a very isolated place," Foudy said, so he tells everyone who works at the newspaper to pass on what they hear. "If you see something that you think is a story, call me. Don't think we know about it." Then, he said, the newsroom can make the decision about coverage. The DeRoses as publishers did not interfere with news coverage. He was never told not to write a story because of the connections of the publisher, and he expects that philosophy to continue.[20]

Dynamic Times

One of the first major decisions NNE made as new owner of the *Gazette* was to take the afternoon newspaper to morning publication. Foudy, who has been at the *Gazette* for more than thirty years, including twenty as editor, said the move had been discussed for years but just never happened. Former Circulation Director Dennis Skoglund, now publisher of the *Greenfield Recorder*, the Gazette's sister publication, and director of operations for the *Gazette*, led the initiative, crunched circulation data, compared it to the competition, and presented a recommendation by a committee of department managers that said flatly, "We need to go morning."[21] Changing reader habits and the desire to be more aggressively competitive, especially against the *Republican* in Springfield, owned by Newhouse, made 2006 the right time for the change. "From my sense of the paper's strengths, from my understanding of how a.m. is going to really capture diverse readership, I feel like this is the right time," Foudy said.[22]

Skoglund tracked circulation data for a decade and found downward trends, like most newspapers, that added up to hefty losses over the years. A good percentage of those losses—30 percent over eight to ten years—were coming from single-copy sales. The *Gazette* had experimented with moving deadlines from early afternoon to late morning and seen an improvement. So Skoglund is confident the decision to move to morning publication will drive single-copy sales higher and make the newspaper delivery more consistent with changing reader habits and lifestyles. In addition, there will be considerably more opportunities for morning single-copy sales. "I strongly feel like it's the right thing to do for the long-term survival and benefit of the *Gazette*."[23]

It will not be an easy transition internally. Both Foudy and Skoglund face the challenges of repositioning staff to make it happen. This is "one of the most unnerving times because I know it's going to be hard on some people," Foudy said. "I have some terrific editors, and I don't want to lose those people. So we're doing some really creative work in terms of the scheduling."[24]

For Skoglund, the issue in large part is the youth who carry the *Gazette*. Distribution is set up geographically. "We have 250 youth carriers, 26 adult motor carriers, and 6 bundle handlers," he said. The change was scheduled to take place in the fall because of the extra hour of daylight saving time. The minimum age limit for youth carriers is nine, but no one under fourteen can legally deliver before 6 a.m. So the decision was made for delivery to have two deadlines: Adults will deliver before 6 a.m., and youth carriers will have a delivery deadline of 6:45 a.m. "Our sister paper in Greenfield has done that, and they've been relatively successful as far as keeping youth carriers. So we're going to try that," he said. He expects, however, to eventually transition to all adult carriers. Skoglund said the *Gazette*'s subscribers have come to expect porch or in-door delivery, a service offered for everyone except those on motor routes, who have tubes. He said porch and door delivery is easier to accomplish with youth carriers. To get adult carriers to offer that kind of customer service, "you're going to have to pay through your nose." From adults, it is typically "bag and toss." Youth routes are smaller than adult routes, too. "We have 6,800 papers that are delivered by youth carriers, and the rest of it is delivered by adults."

The *Gazette* has no ego circulation even though expansion has been tried in the past. "When the *Holyoke Daily Transcript* went out of business back in the early nineties, we opened up home delivery in South Hadley and Granby, and we grew those numbers to a point," Skoglund said. "Then editorial support fell off through the years, and circulation fell off. It's kind of leveled off now at about half what it was at its peak." The *Gazette* also opened distribution to a couple of hill towns in the region. "But I just couldn't make it work to where financially it was worth it, so I ended up cutting it off after about eighteen months," he said. Today the *Gazette* covers nearly all of Hampshire County, a footprint Skoglund is happy with.

About 96 percent of all subscriptions now are paid in advance, and the *Gazette*, like most newspapers, is pushing automatic renewal or easy pay. "We are at almost 20 percent of our home deliveries on easy pay now. It's continuing to grow because we continue to promote it," Skoglund said. Other promotions include a strong Newspaper in Education program, kiosk sales, and promotions at grocery stores, Walmart, and the mall in Hadley. New telemarketing laws had a significantly negative impact on new sales with an estimated 72 percent of the *Gazette*'s market signing up for Do-Not-Call lists. "It's horrible," Skoglund said. "That's where we used to get most of our orders, and now we hardly get anything from telemarketing. That's probably one of the biggest challenges on the circulation side, is how you make those orders up."

There are no sales quotas at the *Gazette* like there are at large corporations. Skoglund agreed with Julien that content has to sell the paper. "The editorial department and advertising are probably more responsible for the numbers in circulation. We can sell it and we can deliver it, but we can't force the people to read the paper. If we're sampling and getting the paper in the home and delivering it with pretty good service, then it's the product that has to sell itself and keep it there."[25]

Circulation at the *Gazette* is about 18,000 Monday to Friday and about 21,000 on Saturday.[26] The circulation director said about 560 pay for online subscriptions, priced at ninety-nine dollars a year. Newspaper websites "have had more of an impact on circulation than what a lot of folks want to admit," Skoglund said. There has been significant impact on home delivery but more on single-copy sales, especially by the occasional reader who buys the newspaper two or three times a week.

Price increases have been used periodically to increase revenue. Four months after the ownership change, the price was raised fifteen cents, the first increase since 1995. Skoglund said, "We did not have one stop—zero." No one called to say they stopped the newspaper because of the price increase.[27]

Elliott, the advertising director, said ad rates have been raised nominally—2 or 3 percent—in the last couple of years, but there has been no significant negative reaction. Advertisers "really complain about advertising rates when the quality of the paper, of the reproduction, of editorial and circulation are all declining and you're charging more," Elliott said. One way to keep complaints down, he has found, is to offer superior customer service. The *Gazette* has an Advertising Service Department, fairly uncommon at newspapers, he said. That allows the sales reps to be on the road more and for the newspaper to still have someone available for the customer to talk to if the sales rep is out. "So we have a high level of customer service, and the quality of the ads we produce is pretty good. ... We're able to provide high value to the advertiser where our rates generally aren't an issue," Elliott said. National advertising is not strong at the *Gazette*, as is the case at other smaller newspapers. Instead, they focus on local advertising "because that's the advertising that you can affect," Elliott said. The result is stable growth without dramatic economic fluctuations. Being located in a college community also "buffers any newspaper from a lot of economic ups and downs," he said.

Keeping that stability is part of the *Gazette*'s business model. "We are not promotion driven in advertising," Elliott said. For example, "at a MediaNews or a Gannett [newspaper], if you're having a bad month, then you do full pages for five hundred dollars, and you have these blips in revenue, but they're not sustainable because they're only based on a price promotion," Elliott said.[28]

Unlike chain newspapers, the *Gazette* has ad proofing built into the system. Most corporate-owned newspapers will say they do not need to pay someone to proof, instead relying on artists or ad salespeople to do the job. But that system has repercussions, Elliott said. "We do have mistakes, but nothing compared to other places where I've worked where people are unhappy and rushed and want to get out of there or are overworked." If an artist works on a vendor tab or special section and puts a tremendous effort into the look of the piece to make it successful, that sells additional similar sections, he said.

One salesperson at the *Gazette* focuses on selling vendor tabs. She researches who in the community is having an anniversary or is building a new building, events that lend themselves to proactive advertising sales. About eighty advertising-driven tabs are produced a year. In addition to sponsorships of events, the *Gazette* attends trade shows for branding and to keep the *Gazette* name visible. "Clearly we jump on anything" that has potential, Elliott said. The free classified ad program is called Aunt Clara's Closet, which is used for items for sale priced under fifty dollars. Craigslist is growing but not overwhelming the market. Employment ads indisputably have migrated to the Internet, but because the newspaper is still "hyperlocal," people are still by far going to a newspaper to look for jobs or to place local employment ads.[29] The newspaper also produces several special sections annually in addition to the advertorial products.

What Lies Ahead?

As the *Gazette* opens its new chapter of ownership, Julien said smaller family newspapers are doing well today, in fact better than major metros, because they have a clear understanding of their mission and their circulation. The majority of stock in the company has been placed in trusts, and inheritance tax issues have been dealt with for the next one hundred years. "I'm running the company to have my kids—and my cousins and nieces and nephews—to have them as thoughtful owners down the road," Julien said. Seventy-five years from now: "That's the time frame I'm looking at."[30]

Notes

1 Peter DeRose (former publisher, *Daily Hampshire Gazette*), interview with the author, May 25, 2006.
2 DeRose, interview.
3 George O'Brien, "Pending Sale of the Gazette Comes at A Challenging Time for Newspapers," *BusinessWest*, http://businesswest.com/details.asp?id=388.
4 Aaron Julien (former publisher, *Daily Hampshire Gazette*), interview with the author, May 25, 2006.
5 DeRose, interview.
6 Jim Foudy (publisher, *Daily Hampshire Gazette*), interview with the author, May 25, 2006.
7 Mark Elliott (advertising director, *Daily Hampshire Gazette*), interview with the author, May 25, 2006.
8 Priscilla Flynn (controller, *Daily Hampshire Gazette*), interview with the author, May 25, 2006.
9 DeRose, interview.
10 Foudy, interview.
11 Flynn, interview.
12 Elliott, interview.
13 Foudy, interview.
14 Flynn, interview.
15 Foudy, interview.
16 Julien, interview.
17 DeRose, interview.
18 Foudy, interview.
19 Julien, interview.
20 Foudy, interview.
21 Dennis Skoglund (former circulation director, *Daily Hampshire Gazette*), interview with the author, May 25, 2006.
22 Foudy, interview.
23 Skoglund, interview.
24 Foudy, interview.
25 Skoglund, interview.
26 Julien, interview.
27 Skoglund, interview.
28 Elliott, interview.
29 Elliott.
30 Julien, interview.

Tulsa World

I t's a different world at the *Tulsa World*. There are no formal budgets to meet. The circulation director routinely consults with the publisher. The operations director feels free to call the president at home—even wake him up—if the need arises. The *Tulsa World* has been run by the Lorton family for one hundred years, and there is a world of difference between this independent and its peer newspapers owned by publicly traded media companies.

Most strikingly different is the company culture at the *World*, simply described as one of intense loyalty to the family, the company, and the community. Employees show their trust and commitment by longevity in service and low turnover. In their world, there is an intimacy and personal connection to management, uncommon at large chain-owned newspapers. Employees say they know what the owners want and are committed to keeping the newspaper successful and, most importantly, in the family.

"I like to believe that everybody that's in a key role in this company is here for two reasons: one, because the management likes the job they do, and two, because they love this company," said Steve Barlow, director of operations.[1]

The Beginnings

The *World* began on September 14, 1905, when J. R. Brady and James F. Mc-Coy published the first edition as the afternoon *Tulsa Daily World*. Eugene Lorton inaugurated the beginning of the Lorton family ownership of the *World* in 1917. Robert E. Lorton, Eugene Lorton's grandson, was named publisher in 1988, and he passed the baton to his son, Robert E. Lorton III, in 2005.[2] The *World* became the only daily newspaper in Tulsa in 1992 when a long-standing joint operating agreement (JOA) between the *World* and the *Tulsa Tribune* was dissolved and the *Tribune* folded.[3] The newspaper in 2005 counted a daily circulation of 150,000.[4]

The World Today

The newspaper has four shareholders and a clear agenda "to make Tulsa healthy," said Robert E. Lorton III, publisher. Lorton said he thinks his community cares that the *World* is locally owned. "We're in the top twenty in readership for a paper our size," he said, due in part to the focus on local content—"our franchise"—but also because "we contribute on average between $1 million and $2 million a year in actual cash back into charities in the marketplace."[5] Philanthropy has been a family tradition, and even in lean times, the company runs free ads for nonprofit events and supports organizations such as United Way, senior services, and the arts. "At independent newspapers, you're concentrating on making your town more livable," Lorton said. "You have to do those things."

Lorton said the key to the *World*'s success is the owners' connection to the community. Citizens have a sense of ownership of the newspaper. They treat it like their product, he said. Even when they call to complain that the newspaper is wet or late, they are passionate about it. Lorton nourishes that connection. "We try to push things that we feel are smart for Tulsa, because when Tulsa is successful we're successful." As an independent, he believes if Tulsa grows, the *World* grows. About 95 percent of the revenue at the *World* comes from the local marketplace, "so if we're not growing as a market, our business is not growing." Retailers don't look at markets that are stagnant or shrinking, but those that are growing. At public corporations, like Gannett for instance, there is constant pressure to squeeze as much as possible into the bottom line, and the popular way to do that is to cut corners to make the next quarter look better than the last. "They're not thinking long term," Lorton said. "We definitely think long term. Not a year; we're thinking two and five years. Where do we want to be? What are we going to do? ... I could make my CFO very happy in the short period by cutting news hole, cutting staff, doing more wire stories, but that does a disservice to our community."

One difference Lorton sees between an independent owner and a publicly owned newspaper is what is deemed the top priority. It is obviously important to make a profit, but that is not always the number one goal. Keeping the stock price up and leaving the impression that the company is growing is paramount for public companies, and it is not uncommon for them to set a goal of growing revenue by 10 percent year to year. Options to meet that goal might include raising rates and cutting costs, but those have damaging long-term effects. Lorton said these companies logically resort to buying more newspapers. "You go in there, you purchase something, you make it a little bit leaner, pay off the debt, and you keep growing the revenue at the same time."

At the *World*, the focus is on long-term value. Journalism and good business do not have to be in opposition to each other, but if the company's focus is on short-term results and higher profits, the methods used to get there can have devastating effects on good journalism. Companies must be willing to reinvest in the business. The *World* bought a new press that Lorton said won't guarantee new revenue but will improve the quality of the product.

At an independent newspaper company, the profit goes directly to the local owners rather than the corporate headquarters, which oftentimes is in another state. The importance of generating a profit is unquestioned, but the issue is how the profit is used. At the *World*, a Sub S corporation, meaning taxes are paid by the shareholders, company profit goes either to the community through charity giving or back into the business. "Every year there's so much we have to purchase, whether we're buying something small such as new digital cameras, or a new computer system, or on a larger scale, mailroom or pressroom equipment. Those are always coming down the road, so if you're not holding back some of that cash, you're going to have to borrow," Lorton said. He said he's happy if he makes 20 percent annual profit while some publicly owned newspapers, driven by Wall Street expectations, pull in much higher percentages. Having a healthy bottom line helps cover the tremendous expense of running a newspaper, but a local owner should be the one who controls how the profit is used—not distant managers or investors.

Streamlined Operations

Unlike most large corporations, the *World* does not set budgets or goals— "never have," Lorton said. But they do watch expenses. "We want all the department heads to still look at their expenses, and if there's a need to purchase something we talk to them about it." It is the nature of companies to go through business cycles, including down business cycles, and higher costs continually lurk around the corner—soaring fuel prices, for instance. "We always strive to be better the next year, and we always strive to put out a better product tomorrow." The lack of a budget does not mean the company ignores performance measures. "We compare everything to where we were last year, same month. ... Then we ask questions: Why was so-and-so down 15 percent last month? And we go talk to the advertiser or the salesperson. ... It could be as simple as their [an advertiser's] business is suffering so they're down."[6]

An efficient system allows more hands-on management and faster decision making. Barlow said the operational structure speeds up the whole operation and is better for everyone. "If I need a decision made that I feel uncomfortable going out on a limb for, or if I want to consult with the president of the company, he's twenty-five feet down the hall. I don't have to make a call to New York City and wait three days to talk to somebody."[7] In a company the size of the *World*, Barlow is comfortable calling the publisher at home. An independent newspaper brings a level of intimacy and trust lacking at publicly owned companies. Loyalty from the staff sets the *World* apart. Most people who work there "love this place," Barlow said. "They love this family they work for. We're not in a unique industry, but we might be in some ways a unique company within that industry." With the exception of a few employees who work solely for a paycheck, he said, "you won't find a more dedicated group of managers, and you won't find a more dedicated group of employees either. I think that speaks highly for this company and the ownership of it."

At a publicly owned company, loyalty oftentimes is missing because employees move around and their current position is viewed as a stepping stone to their next. "I'm not saying people in those big companies don't have a measure of loyalty, but their loyalty is to the corporate headquarters that pays them and keeps them on the payroll," Barlow said. "Here we don't live in fear that next month we're going to have to pull up stakes and move our entire family across the country. There's nowhere to go. This is the place. This is the only place."

It may be cliché to say the *World* is a family atmosphere, but it is true. Beyond the Lortons, other families work at the newspaper, a characteristic more common in businesses decades ago. Barlow's mother, father, and grandfather were all *World* employees as was his wife. His daughters and son-in-law also worked there. There are several other examples of family employment, and there is no mandatory retirement age. One employee retired at age eighty-two after fifty-five years with the company. Barlow said the culture of loyalty stems from the Lorton legacy. "Bobby is a part of that legacy," he said, describing a hands-on management style and regular involvement with employees. Lorton regularly visits all departments and is not aloof like some top executives. But more than anything else, he is accessible. Lorton periodically holds what are called "brown bags," informal question-and-answer forums with employees. "It's a great way to communicate with people," Barlow said. "Memos are fantastic, and they save a lot of meeting time, but nothing beats the president of the company sitting down in a chair with you, looking at you with his hands behind his head and saying, 'What do you want to know?' "[8]

Joe Worley, executive editor, said Lorton's "State of the World" forums, which are longer question-and-answer sessions that start in the newsroom and make the rounds to other departments, are opportunities for employees to find out about the company and Lorton's plans for the future. "He's pretty open about his vision of the business that we're in—the information business," Worley said. "That's where he sees it."[9]

Worley said the family is committed to the concept that they have to produce a product people want to buy, and they recognize that to do that they have to invest in the product. At a public company, local editors oftentimes have bureaucracies to navigate to sell ideas, frequently to top executives they do not know well. "I know Bobby Lorton, and I know Bob Lorton. And I may not get the answer that I want every time, but at least I'm going to get an answer, and I'm going to get it pretty quick. I'm not going to have to play the corporate game," Worley said.

Cutting expenses is not reserved only for tough times. Barlow said at the *World*, all employees are dedicated to keeping tight control of expenses. Managers continually seek ideas that can save dollars without compromising quality. The trend at newspapers to buy the cheapest paper and ink hurts their product, but they are willing to give up quality for profit, he said. "Many of our materials are not the cheapest thing we could get. We buy the thing that gives us the best quality, gives us the best print job, the best looking newspaper." He said the *World* does not scrimp, but employees do what is needed to maintain an income level that allows the bills to be paid and some profit to be locked away for future use.[10]

As the industry has tightened, strategic moves have been implemented at the *World* as at other newspapers to minimize the impact of a downturn. Staff cuts, one of the most popular strategies to lower expenses at public companies, are less likely at the *World*. Resisting staff cuts for most of the newspaper's history led Lorton to consider other options. His philosophy was to cut if absolutely necessary in areas that have no impact on the product and are unlikely to be noticed by customers. Out of a newsroom of 160, he said about 2 positions were eliminated. Instead, the janitorial staff was trimmed, which affected about 30 people, and that operation was outsourced. Cutting news hole is always another option, and it was trimmed at the *World* not long ago from 70 percent to 60 percent. Vowing not to go below 60 percent, Lorton said it is not uncommon in the industry today to see a 40 percent news hole. But, "I think it's too much of a gamble to cut your news hole." Often readers will not realize that something has been cut, but over the long term the product gets stale and boring. "That's why the local side is so critical, because that's what we do," he said.[11]

Worley said the newsroom started looking at some features they could eliminate, the kid's corner, for instance, and different ways to provide local information to readers. Reporters write shorter stories, and the newsroom is more selective about the stories they cover. Ultimately, he said, he thinks it's a good exercise to periodically reevaluate content. "When you go for fifteen years and you've never had to ask yourself questions, it's probably healthy that you do. But by the same token, I can see some days when I pick up the paper and I say, 'Geez, this is awfully tight.' There were some other stories that didn't get into today's paper that I wish we'd been able to do."[12] The focus in the newsroom today is on the kind of product they are putting out and how much they are spending to do it. Worley said he thinks the surviving niche for independent newspapers is being able to provide local news. The print form of the newspaper has a future, but "will our circulation be as large as it is today? Probably not. I think there is a huge market out there online. But there'll always be a print [product], a portable form that you can pick up and take with you," he said.

Raising the price of the newspaper is another popular way to increase revenue, and the *World* uses that strategy, too. During the JOA with the *Tribune*, it was difficult to raise prices because "every time we raised our price ... it really hurt them," Lorton said.[13] But once the contract was bought out, they decided to move up the monthly subscription rates. It took ten years to double the price of the newspaper. "We went from $6.50 to $12.00," Lorton said. "Now we're at almost $15.00, and I still say newspapers hurt themselves when they don't raise their subscription prices, because we are basically saying the value is not there." Today, the strategy is to raise the price $0.30 a month once a year. He tells complaining readers, "It's a penny a day increase," and they typically realize that is not so bad. "What can you get delivered to your house for $0.50?" he asks. "So our revenue in circulation has doubled even though we have less circulation today." He does not believe it is smart to continue to raise advertising rates. "The subscriber eventually has to take some of that load if they want a good product."

Daily Production

The *World* started cutting back on ego circulation, or distribution to areas that cost more than the revenue they bring in, after 2000 when management decided it did not make sense from a business standpoint to subsidize circulation in areas that were extremely costly just to have a presence there. But before that, it was just about the numbers. The newspaper took the bold step in 2001 to get out of the Audit Bureau of Circulations (ABC) and they stayed out for three or four years, Bill King, circulation director, said. However, they kept ABC-type guidelines and had an outside auditor come in for an audit.[14] Also in 2001, like most newspapers, the *World* switched from carrier collection to total office pay. The benefits were more accurate counts of their subscribers and fewer carrier-route turnovers. "We went to 100 percent office pay, and now we know who all our customers are and what they're paying. And the carriers like it because now they don't have to collect," Lorton said.[15]

Today, rising gas prices are a major problem. The Circulation Department created a scale based on a range of gas prices. Then they figured out how many miles were traveled on each route and grouped those routes into five categorizes. If gas falls between a certain price range, the company pays what is called a fuel adjustment. If it goes below a certain range, there is no adjustment. "It was something we had to scramble to get together when things started getting really bad," King said.[16] "But now that it's in place, it's nice to have it because if fuel drops down to a certain level, it's not an issue. If it goes back up, we've already got something in place that will help." The adjustment is paid twice a month. When gas prices started soaring, the newspaper also gave their carriers an across-the-board increase. A benefit of that increase was "that it allowed us to pick a little higher base for our scale," he said.

King said the newspaper's complaint percentage of carrier delivery is low in part because good customer service is a high priority at the newspaper. "If you're late here and there, they [the customers] know it's just not a normal situation," he said. The Circulation Department's delivery times have been helped by the new presses, which are faster and more efficient, even though the *World* has later delivery times than is common. The daily production window starts at midnight and ends at 3 a.m. The timeline requires all deliveries to be on the doorstep by 6 a.m. in the full distribution area, including outlying areas. For Sundays with a larger distribution area and longer pressrun, the production window ends at 4 a.m. with a 7 a.m. delivery time. Barlow said the press foreman has standing orders to call him if there is the possibility that the newspaper will be late. On rare occasions when it happens, the circulation director notifies his field workers, and local radio and television stations are sent a news release.[17] A further step involves the phone system. "If we are running into mechanical problems or weather related [difficulties], we've created five or six different types of [recorded] messages on our phone system just to let people know," King said.

Porching the newspaper is offered, though not promoted. King said in the past, carriers porched the newspaper for elderly or handicapped subscribers. But in the last several years, if a customer requests it, the carrier will comply.

The majority of carriers are adults, and the average route size is 300 papers. In previous years, some carriers were delivering 600–800 papers, but the Circulation Department felt that was too large, so today no routes larger than 300–315 papers are allowed with the exception of a few that were grandfathered in. Most routes take two to two-and-a-half hours to deliver.

Addressing the wet newspaper complaint can be a challenge, but King said there are solutions. He said they get fewer complaints when the paper is thrown on the grass at the edge of the driveway or sidewalk. Some customers, though, prefer driveway or sidewalk delivery. Carriers are asked to double bag on wet days, and all papers on Sunday are bagged. As for service percentage, which is based on complaints per thousand, "on a daily, we're averaging probably .6 to .8 per thousand, and on Sundays, we're averaging about 1.4, 1.5. So our service, we feel—and we seem to hear it from the customers—is really good," King said.

The lack of a budget is not an open checkbook for the Circulation Department, King said. "We have to watch our expense just like anybody else, and we have to generate revenue" even though a circulation department is not usually high revenue generating. His is, however, because of promotions and the way they manage expenses. There are fewer levels of management, "so we're lean, but we're efficient," he said.

The award-winning Newspaper in Education Department was started about fifteen years ago, and the *World* has made a commitment to develop it into a high-quality program. There are also subscriber discounts. A weekender discount is offered for Friday to Sunday subscriptions as well as three-month, six-month, and yearly discounts. Two or three years ago, the newspaper eliminated its telemarketing and youth door-knocking crews. "At the time we were thinking, 'Oh man, is that suicide or what?' ... Fortunately, we had enough foresight where we knew with the telemarketing laws that was going to be a struggle. So we actually did that a year before it became an issue," King said. Outside contractors were hired to replace the youth door-knocking crews. A carrier-sampling program proved highly successful with a retention rate as high as 70–80 percent. Fliers were sent out with sample papers to five addresses per carrier on Monday, Tuesday, and Wednesday. Then another five addresses were targeted on Thursday, Friday, and Saturday. A high-dollar promotion vehicle was developed to take the *World* brand to events like Mayfest or the opening of Bass Pro. Today there is in-house telemarketing to "people we've done business with over the last twelve to fifteen months."

King said he is proud of the fact that until two years ago there were never any layoffs at the company. When it did happen, circulation lost only about six employees. Company-wide, he estimates there were forty or so out of about seven hundred employees at the time. Today, about six hundred people work at the *World*. The Lortons have been generous in raises and benefits, King said. "They're a great, great group of people to work for."[18] Meeting with the president and publisher routinely once a week sets the *World* apart from a big corporate newspaper. "The family is here, they're active in the day-to-day production of the product and management of the product, and [they are] involved in the community. That is the big key with a family owned newspaper," said Bill Carr, state/traffic manager. "You know what the management philosophy is. You know what they want."[19]

The Future

Lorton is optimistic about the future of print journalism and newspapers because of their local franchise. In ten years, he sees the *World* more like it is today. Acknowledging the impact of the Internet on the industry, he said it has hurt readership. But it is uncomfortable for readers to read long stories on today's computers, phones, or personal digital assistants. And until someone invents better technology, newspapers will continue to be viable and read. There also is the advantage of thumbing through a newspaper and finding headlines that catch the eye and lead readers to unexpected new and interesting information. "I don't see that going away," he said. "As long as people care about their community, then I think newspapers have a future. Bottom line, we are in the newspaper business, but we really are in the information business. As long as people want that information, the newspaper is the one source that can gather it."

Readers will also recognize a brand for news they believe in and come back to that brand—whether it is in a print product or on the Internet. "We're lucky we have a brand that people trust. Trust is very important in producing a paper," Lorton said. Readers have to trust the product and try it, and advertisers have to trust that it will bring in customers. Newspapers have a future because citizens have trust and faith in them. "I think the printed product, until someone invents a laptop or some other new device that is flexible and is affordable, is going to be hard to beat," he said.

But the *World* is looking to grow the website because it has viable uses. With improving technology, research and development, the *World* is focused on finding products that better reach readers' needs and go beyond the typical print categories of news, sports, entertainment, and classifieds.

The *World* initially started with a bulletin board, then went to a free website managed by a third party. Realizing the company needed more control, they brought the website in house and designated a staff to run it, growing to twenty-five employees at one time. But it was a bad model, Lorton said. "We had programmers, and this built up over five years and revenue was growing. But for every dollar I was bringing in, it was costing me three dollars." At one point, he estimated he was losing a half-million dollars a year on it. So in the interest of improved efficiency and cooperation, Lorton gave the newsroom ownership of tulsaworld.com, a move he said was the best decision he made. He also cut staff and converted to a paid site, making the *World* one of the first newspapers to take that critical step, because they were losing subscribers to the print product. Readers were reading the newspaper free online. "I went to our web publisher and said, 'I'm charging fifty cents on the street for the print product, and they're quitting and going online and reading it for free. It doesn't make sense for me to gather the stories, edit it, and put it out in a readable form and then give it away for free out the back door." Lorton said at first he got plenty of calls from angry readers complaining about the paid subscriptions. "I would write back and politely say, 'I understand where you're coming from. But we have a business still to run, and I'm losing subscribers because of letting this out for free. If you can get this information elsewhere, then so be it.' But I knew they couldn't." In 2006, the *World* lifted the restrictions on the website and began offering tulsaworld.com and stories from the archives for free.

CNN is the model for content today on the *World*'s website, Lorton said. "This is our page, and we don't have it real cluttered. If you click on a story, we may have an ad there. We're trying to copy more of what CNN has done" including streaming videos, links to stories, and sponsoring pages.

Acquiring another newspaper could be in the future for the company. Lorton said he looks at growing the company by buying smaller newspapers in the 20,000–30,000 circulation range. Those papers would not have to be in their current marketplace. Though considerably larger in circulation than what he has envisioned, the best opportunity for the *World* would be buying the *Daily Oklahoman* in Oklahoma City if it were to come on to the market. "That would make sense for us because we could actually justify paying more for it because of the savings we would see" in covering University of Oklahoma sports, for example. "But the first thing I would do with the *Oklahoman*," Lorton said, "is I would take this half of the state and they would take the other half. I would say, 'Forget this ego circulation,' and we'd get down to delivering the paper to where it makes sense for the advertisers and the reader."

Not a fan of convergence, Lorton has resisted overtures from two local television stations for partnerships because he does not see how a partnership would increase circulation and revenue. He has the same philosophy with cross ownership. Because of bundling ad packages across mediums, Lorton said a company ends up cutting rates and competing with itself if they own more than one media outlet in a market. So savings on the news-gathering side would be nil. He said the *Oklahoman* partners with Channel 9 in Oklahoma City. "But I told the guy who owns Channel 6 here in town, 'The day the *Oklahoman* circulation goes up because they're partners with you, I'll listen to you.' When a newspaper partners with a television station, their ratings will benefit more than your circulation because your coverage is so much larger than theirs." The only thing that would make him embrace convergence would be if the move would grow newspaper circulation, and he said he has not seen an instance of that.

Clustering—designed to save money for a newspaper company by printing several newspapers at a central printing site—is successful at saving money, but it does not fill the needs of the communities. "You still need somebody there in those local towns to cover those local issues," Lorton said. Nearly two-thirds of the *World*'s advertising revenue comes from local advertisers. "It is important for us to cultivate those mom and pops and to keep them in the paper because we don't want them to go out of business."

Lorton said the *World* has remained independent despite offers over the years simply because the owners do not want to sell. With two sisters, neither of whom is interested in running the newspaper, the future of the *World* may be up to Lorton and the next generation. He has three children, his oldest sister has two, and his middle sister has three. "It takes some family members still wanting to work here," he said. Lorton and his sisters all have equal stock in the company, and his father's philosophy was that whoever works at the newspaper should get paid a salary. Lorton thinks it is important for whoever is running the business to have control of the voting stock and the authority to make daily operational decisions. They must also think long term and not "shoot the golden goose" as many families do. Keeping peace in the family is achieved by being fair with one another. "The only thing that would probably make us sell is if I got tired of the business. And the decision would have to be, does anyone else want to do it?"

Had he not returned to Tulsa from Colorado where he went to college, his father may have put the newspaper out for bid when he decided to retire. Families faced with huge estate taxes, and family members unwilling to take on the task of preserving the family legacy at the newspaper, sometimes are forced to sell. But Lorton said the family has been smart about estate planning and they really like the business. If he sold, he said he wonders what he would do. "I wouldn't move out of this marketplace. I like Tulsa. We have places to go visit and vacation places, but we still always choose to live here. We like the community." Ultimately, though, "you have to enjoy what you do, period."[20]

The Associated Press reported in January 2009 that the *World* cut 5 percent of its workforce. Lorton said in a statement to employees, "Just because this is the prudent business decision, it is not any less difficult. ... It's a story that's been played out across the city and country as businesses are faced with the unpleasant responsibility of adjusting their payrolls in this harsh economic downturn." In 2008, the newspaper eliminated its weekly Community World editions as part of its cost-savings strategy.[21]

Notes

1 Steve Barlow (director of operations, *Tulsa World*), interview with the author, Oct. 20, 2005.
2 Randy Krehbiel, "Tulsa World," Oklahoma Historical Society's Encyclopedia of Oklahoma History and Culture, http://digital.library.okstate.edu/encyclopedia/entries/T/TU017.html/.
3 *Tulsa World*, "Tribune to Close Sept. 30," *Tulsa World*, July 31, 1992, http://www.tulsaworld.com/news/article.aspx?no=subj&articleid=337201&archive=yes.
4 Robert E. Lorton III (publisher, *Tulsa World*), interview with the author, Oct. 20, 2005.
5 Lorton, interview.
6 Lorton.
7 Barlow, interview.
8 Barlow.
9 Joe Worley (executive editor, *Tulsa World*), interview with the author, Oct. 20, 2005.
10 Barlow, interview.
11 Lorton, interview.
12 Worley, interview.
13 Lorton, interview.
14 Bill King (circulation director, *Tulsa World*), interview with the author, Oct. 20, 2005.
15 Lorton, interview.
16 King, interview.
17 Barlow, interview.
18 King, interview.
19 Bill Carr (state/traffic manager, *Tulsa World*), interview with the author, Oct. 20, 2005.
20 Lorton, interview.
21 Justin Juozapavicius, Associated Press, "Newspaper lays off 28," Jan. 6, 2009.

10

The Gazette in Cedar Rapids

From the sweet morning smells of the Quaker Oats cereal factory, to the brisk wind and crusty snow, Cedar Rapids is an all-American city. It is quintessentially midwestern—friendly, close-knit, and responsible with strong family values. So it's no surprise that for 124 years the family owned *Gazette* in Cedar Rapids has greeted Eastern Iowans with its unique brand of homegrown journalism. "When you live in a community, you have to take responsibility for it," said Joe Hladky, Gazette Company chairman.[1]

A sense of responsibility and pride lie at the heart of the newspaper's mission in its community. They also guide employees' mission inside the newspaper. Until 2006, descendants of the Faulkes and Miller families had managed the *Gazette*. Chuck Peters, the first nonfamily member to lead the company, was named president and CEO in 2006. An employee stock ownership plan (ESOP) was created in 1986 as part of the company's benefits program. Employees in January 2006 owned about 33 percent of the newspaper stock,[2] a factor that has helped the *Gazette* stave off acquisition by huge media companies. "I get approached about twice a week," Hladky said.[3]

What Is Different?

Elbridge T. Otis and Lucian H. Post, owners of weekly newspapers in DeKalb and Rochelle, Illinois, published the first *Evening Gazette* in Cedar Rapids on January 10, 1883. But within the first year, they sold the newspaper to Fred Faulkes and his brother-in-law, Clarence Miller. Cedar Rapids at the time was a city of about 15,000, and the *Gazette* sold about 1,200 papers daily for three cents each.[4] Today, Cedar Rapids has a population of 120,758, a metropolitan-area population of 191,701, and the *Gazette* has a daily circulation of 60,739 and a Sunday circulation of 75,365.[5]

Hladky said the *Gazette* struggled during the early days when there were up to ten other newspapers in the city, but the will to survive prevailed. "I take familial pride in that," he said. "What we do in the community benefits the community and at the same time [it] benefits us. We're everyplace in this community," contributing financially, volunteering, and producing a strong editorial product. The employee ownership structure also builds pride, he said, giving an example of a request from the newspaper's Community Affairs Department for forty volunteers for an upcoming charity event. Without question, plenty of employees will show up, he said.[6]

The *Gazette* corporate mission statement focuses on community: "Our mission is to be the information provider of choice through a dynamic mix of innovative products and services. We will create and maintain mutually beneficial, long-term relationships with our customers, employees and the communities we serve."[7]

Peg Schmitz, general manager and vice president of operations, explains that attitudes and business practices within the company make the *Gazette* different. Having a publisher who is the key decision maker on site and having sensitivity in the community are critical. "We really do associate ourselves with the community," she said. "The mindset is different. I think there is much more balanced coverage because you have to answer to the people in the community. You're a part of the community and much more concerned about those things that a larger newspaper organization might not want to pursue because you realize the impact on the community."

At some newspapers, family ownership can mean a lack of focus on the business or a strong business model as well as a reluctance to change processes that have been in place for years. Schmitz said at the *Gazette*, however, there is strong awareness of the need to be competitive and that solid business practices are important. "But there's still heart," she said. "We'll make tough decisions when we have to, but there is still a sense of where you are in the community, your visibility, and that people have been here a long time and are very loyal."

The ownership team runs the show. Managers across the business units work in collaboration. On small capital expenditures within an operational unit, decisions are made within the group. But if decisions affect other groups, there is discussion. "It's very collaborative," Schmitz said. There has to be a high degree of trust and respect for what everybody brings to the table and a desire to keep people in the collaborative process.

The ESOP ownership structure enhances that collaboration. All employees have access to the publisher. Schmitz said employees take ownership pride in the *Gazette* as their business, and with that comes responsibility for smart business decisions. They have learned to think more universally than their own departments and to make a commitment to the big picture. "So a lot of it is just their general commitment," she said. "That means I have ownership. I make the tough decisions. I reap some of the benefits. [We're] trying to instill a sense of ownership."[8]

Gazette Ownership

In 1914, Harry L. Marshall, foreman of the composing room and later editor, bought one-third interest in the newspaper from the Faulkes family.[9] In 1986 when Marshall family members wanted to sell their *Gazette* stock, Miller descendants added some shares, and the company created the ESOP. Originally the ESOP stock was valued at $248.50 a share. On December 31, 2006, each share was valued at more than $1,000 per share. In 1986 the ESOP held 44 percent of the company stock, and in January 2005 the plan held about 33 percent. "The percentage of stock eligible employees hold in the plan varies as people retire and sell their allocated shares back to the company," a book on the history of the company by Hladky states. To be eligible for the plan, employees must have been employed for one year in which they worked one thousand hours. They are vested after working at the company for six years. Allocations are made to their account annually and total 4 percent to 5 percent of their annual salary.[10]

All of the family members have common grandparents, and the family ownership today represents those two founding families. In addition to the 33 percent of stock owned by the ESOP, the remainder is owned by the founding families. A half-dozen people control most of that, and Peters said they don't have any desire to sell the newspaper.[11]

Like most family owned newspapers, succession planning is a huge issue. But in Cedar Rapids, fortunately there is a fifth generation family member who is interested in the family business and is now working at the newspaper. Elizabeth Hladky, thirty-two, Joe's daughter, graduated from the University of Iowa in December 1996 and moved to California to work in childcare. A year later, she was persuaded by her father to return to Cedar Rapids because her grandmother, Jane Hladky, was ill.[12] She took a job in the Ad Design Department but didn't like it. "I made photocopies for print ads and had no real interest in the paper whatsoever, but I knew I should work so I did," she said. "Then about a year later, I realized that I was actually bleeding *Gazette* blue, and I moved into management." She got involved with the *Gazette*'s team-training program and "fell in love with the business and developed a passion." She stayed in ad design for about five years as a supervisor, then moved on to operations. In March 2006, she joined the Circulation Department as home delivery manager.[13] "I'm not presuming I'll be the next publisher," she said.[14]

But she said keeping the newspaper in the family is a huge responsibility and a tradition she wants to continue.[15]

The family business under the Gazette Company name has two subsidiaries: Gazette Communications, which includes the newspaper and was incorporated in 1999; and Cedar Rapids Television Company, which includes KCRG-TV9 and KCRG Radio AM (sold in 2006) and was incorporated in 1953. Decisionmark, a company incorporated in 1993 that began as a newspaper mapping service but changed to one that produces high-tech products for the broadcast industry and television viewers, was sold to a broadcast investment group in 2007.[16]

Joe Hladky said there was a time when family companies lived out of their checkbook. If the company had a good year, the family had a good year. If the company had a bad year, it was just that, but it generally wasn't so bad because the company only had to please the family owners. For years at the *Gazette*, there were no annual budgets or department budgets, and there was no strategic planning. Hladky said that when he took over as publisher in 1980, he knew the company needed a formalized operating plan for it to prevail. "We had a philosophy that we were going to run this place as close to a public company as we could and still have compassion while maintaining independence," he said. "We were going to adopt business practices that made sense for our company and our employees. So do we have hard-and-fast rules and set goals and profit margins? To some extent, yes. We have to because if we don't, we don't produce an acceptable profitability. Our stockholders aren't going to live with that very long. It's not rocket science. You've got to perform to stay in business."[17]

Hladky hired Ken Slaughter, chief financial officer, in 1981. He also implemented other changes. The company's first Personnel Department was created in 1975, work was done on formal policies and procedures, and employee newsletters began in 1977. In 1983 the first employee handbook was finished, and in 1985 the first survey of employees' attitudes about the company was completed, followed by quarterly Let's Talk meetings for employees and management. Most significantly perhaps was the establishment of the ESOP in 1986. Today there is a Learning and Development Department as well as training programs, coaching sessions, and an Employee Advisory Council (EAC) "designed as a voice of employees to management, and management to employees." One successful EAC project was a company-wide recycling project that in 2004 recycled 1,326 tons of paper, equivalent to saving 22,548 trees and 118,043 cubic feet of landfill space. The company also has an employee recognition program called Special Thanks and Recognition (STAR), designed to reward outstanding work with merchandise and cash.[18]

Community Ties

For an editor, local ownership can be the best of all possible worlds. Mark Bowden, *Gazette* editor, said the biggest advantage is the owners' familiarity with the community they serve. "You've got owners who know the community, and you have vast institutional knowledge, especially if it's been the same families that have owned the paper for 125 years." The families and the newspaper have grown up together in Cedar Rapids. The city is 150 years old, so the newspaper owners "are deep in the community. They historically have touched and rubbed elbows with the people who have made the community what it is, so they know the history." Because the newspaper is a local business, there's a different and better relationship between the newspaper and the community. "For some reason, there's a little extra credibility," he said.

The downside to local ownership at newspapers, Bowden said, can be a lack of resources and innovation. But if the newspaper is large enough to have the resources to effect change, the downside is having the wherewithal to deal with the rigors of the business. "You end up spreading yourself fairly thin when you're independent, in terms of having to do your own marketing and so forth," he said. "But I think in terms of credibility and American culture today, people still want to know where the buck stops. They want to know who is accountable. And with accountability, you develop credibility. That's what it's all about in the newspaper business."

Customers like the ability to get their complaints or comments to the top. If they can get to the person who signs the paychecks or owns a significant part of the company, it makes a difference to them. "If you're an offsite owner, I'm not sure you'd be much different than the corporates, but if you're here and you have somebody confront you on the street and say, 'Why did you put my drunken-driving arrest in the paper?' or 'Oh, boy, you guys did a great job'—you hear that. I think credibility comes with accessibility, and that's important," Bowden said.

Quality counts, but to an editor, quantity doesn't necessarily equate to quality. Bowden defines quality as the ability of people within an organization to make news judgments about what is important, organize information, prioritize it, and give the community a sense of its importance. "It's not about investigative journalism or the Pulitzer Prize-winning story," he said, even though the *Gazette* won a Pulitzer in 1936 for a series of stories on liquor and political racketeering in Iowa. "It's about the grassroots information. If we can create that sense of community, then we will flourish. And I think what is ironic in this industry is that, for the very reasons that these newspapers were snapped up by chains that were such good investments, they've divested those newspapers of the very assets that made them a great buy and made them a reason that they should be owned." He said somebody somewhere someday will wake up and say, "What we bought yesterday isn't worth as much today because we stripped it of its mettle, its heart and soul." That's a sad commentary, but much of what he said he thinks is going on today.

While newspapers are very different from what they were decades ago, what the public expects of them continues to evolve whether they are corporate owned or independent. Bowden said, "The question will be how close to the mark will they meet the readers' expectations? ... I don't know how much that is talked about in corporate circles. I would say in this company, I'm very proud that our mission statement said that we seek the truth, and that's a part of our culture. We believe that yes, we should be giving the owners a good return on their investment, but we're catalysts in the community, and we have responsibilities in the community."

Reaching the Community

With the goals of connecting with the community, hearing what readers want but still giving readers what they need, the *Gazette* every month for twenty-five years has held community events they call "coffees" in some of the three hundred small communities in their circulation area. They go into the community and do a story on some aspect of the community, and on the day the story runs in the newspaper, some of the newspaper staff show up at the local coffee shop. "We buy coffee and rolls for an hour and a half, and we just talk with people," Bowden said. "We ask for their assessment of the paper." The meetings are informal, and there is no program—just people sitting in a town coffee shop drinking coffee. But Bowden said he and other newsroom staff go and ask the questions: "What are we doing? What are we missing?"

For ten years the *Gazette* has held an annual event called In the Neighborhood. Each summer they do a significant feature on seven to eleven neighborhoods and hold a block party in each. "We provided popcorn and lemonade, and we're out in those neighborhoods for two hours. People came, and there is a discussion of what we're doing," Bowden said.

The *Gazette* holds community forums for candidates for city council. Every year there is a community-wide reading project where staffers read books and look for social issues. One of the recent books was *Hogs in Heaven* about biracial children. Another was *Plainsong*, a fictional piece about a pregnant teenager who ends up living with older people. Reporters are assigned to write stories about the social issues, Bowden said. "We look at these social issues, and we do a lot of reporting, and then we hold public forums and bring in experts to further flesh out the discussion of those social issues."

Many newspapers, especially ones the size of the *Gazette*, do not have an ombudsman, but the *Gazette* had one until about a year ago. They are looking to fill the open position. The former ombudsman, a journalism professor, worked part time and wrote a column every eight weeks. "People thought he was the state ombudsman," Bowden said, because he got many calls from people about problems in the state. He would participate in the news meetings, go to many public events, and people would address all sorts of journalistic issues with him. "If there was a controversial issue out there about the *Gazette*, he would weigh in on it," Bowden said. "He would take us to task if we didn't follow our own policies."

For an editor, local ownership can also mean a mandate to cover stories in which the publisher has a personal interest. But Bowden said that doesn't happen at the *Gazette* despite the publisher's heavy involvement in the community. "Joe and Chuck have served on chamber boards and all kinds of things. They are privy to a lot of information and take those jobs with the expectation that some of that stuff is pretty confidential," Bowden said. Hladky and Peters are not an inside source for the *Gazette*, but reporters and editors have been able to confirm information through them. Bowden said Hladky and Peters take the position that "you do the reporting, and if you can find information from verifiable sources, I'll certainly tell you whether the newspaper is going to be wrong or right if it publishes the story. ... It's a local business. They are local businessmen and care about the community. That's just part of the condition." Peters, who has a background in law and appliance manufacturing, came to the *Gazette* in 1998. He has continued the company commitment to local involvement and also became active with the Newspaper Association of America.

Tough Times

Family owned newspapers are no more immune to tough times than corporate owned ones, and when staff cuts are necessary, they struggle. "No one is immune to cuts," Bowden said. There have been changes in the size of the newspaper. The web width has been reduced. Sections have been added and later dropped, but "there hasn't been a wholesale drop in the news hole by 10 or 20 percent," he said. "If we hired staff for a section and we no longer produce it, then how can we justify keeping the staff? There's always been a propensity to fund and provide the resources needed, but if the direction changes, to also pull the resources back. That's been very helpful, and I think we go into that understanding those things."

A family owned newspaper has more latitude to make quick changes, either to try new products or eliminate those that aren't producing the revenue desired. "It's not like there are changes every day, but I can just think in the past several years where we've tried different things. Some of them have been very successful, some of them marginally successful. If we decided it's not worth the effort, we let it go," Bowden said.

Similarly there have been changes in the number of pressruns. In the past, the *Gazette* published three editions of the newspaper. Today there is a zoned section published three times a week, partly the result of a powerful new press. "In the old days, as the paper was chugging along, you had time to update an edition," Bowden said. "Now we really have one edition with a zoned insert. On any given night there are two pressruns. There's an early run at 7:30 or 8, and that zone section is in that run. Then the late section is the A section, the local section, and the sports section, which are printed around midnight."[19]

Hladky said about five years ago the company offered a voluntary severance program to some older staffers and lost thirty to forty people. Later the company reduced the staff by thirty-five to forty people, and attrition has been used to cut staff. Those decisions along with technology made the newspaper more efficient but may have diminished coverage slightly. "We've had to make some hard decisions," he said. "I'm sure we're not covering some things that we used to, and we've dropped some features ... But I would also maintain that just because we were doing something five years ago doesn't mean that was right. And hard times make you look at those things ... We've cut some things out and not heard a word, so you say, 'Maybe that's OK.' "[20]

Schmitz said if she has to call an employee in and tell him his job has been eliminated, she wants to be able to "respectfully face somebody" and explain how that decision was made. The company tries to find opportunities to transfer employees to other positions elsewhere in the company. "Usually when we've had to downsize it's been four or five positions. And there's a lot of thought that goes into having documentation, assessing skills, assessing business needs. I would say that 50 percent of the time people weren't very surprised. [They say,] 'I saw where my role was shrinking or there wasn't a need for this, or I understand why it might have happened,' " Schmitz said.[21]

In the Circulation Department, staff cuts were handled through early retirement and were voluntary. Scott Swenson, circulation director, said a plus about being independent is "we were able to do it [staff cutbacks] through attrition and take our time. We didn't make it an event. We made it a nine-month process." He said there hasn't been a backlash from staff reductions in his department.[22]

A strong commitment to local news and quality, especially by the publisher, helps direct resources to the news side. "We're never going to get all we need, but I would say that we certainly have an abundance of resources," Bowden said. He thinks editorial has the resources needed to meet and exceed customers' expectations today. "There has been a commitment to that," Bowden said. "Without credible local news in the paper you have a shopper. And without news you no longer have credibility. ... I think we're fortunate that our publisher understands that that's a key. Without credible news, you won't get advertising. And without credible news, who will believe it either?"[23]

New Technology

Keeping up with new technology and being able to integrate it into the company can be difficult for family owned newspapers. "The ability that a large corporate group has to finance, versus us having to finance things out of our own cash flow," is an issue, Hladky said. "We can't go to Sacramento or Tyson's Corner and make a case for a new press or whatever. We've got to do it right here." In July 1999 the *Gazette* began using a new Goss Universal 70 Press. "In the newspaper and television business, which is our core, the technology is almost a sandpit into which your pour water, as far as money goes, to keep technologically there.

"And now we have big dollar investment needs for TV as we convert to digital broadcasting. Normally when you make an investment you say, 'What's the ROI [return on investment]?' The only ROI for the digital investment in our TV station is we get to keep our license. There's not one extra eyeball that comes to you because you're digital. When it comes time to get your license, if you haven't reached the levels of technology that the FCC requires, they're going to give the license to somebody else. So you've got an *x*-million-dollar investment sitting over there and no way to turn it on."

Early on, the *Gazette* made the decision to charge for the "other than headline" parts of their website. The *Gazette* had about five hundred to six hundred online subscriptions before moving away from that model in 2007. Charging for use of its website raised the ire of many in an era where readers think the Internet should be free. The reader reaction to the decision was huge, Hladky said. But he used a standard response to complaints. "I said, 'I don't know of an economic model that allows us to pay the people who put the product on the street if we're giving it away.' Maybe online advertising works for Google or the *New York Times*—I'm not even sure it does for them—but people aren't just rushing to our website to post banner ads and do all that other stuff. It was kind of lonely out there when we first started charging. And it was not a well-received decision here because everybody else was giving it away." By late 2009, a new version of GazetteOnline no longer required readers to set up an account to access the e-edition or the company's e-mail newsletters.[24]

Hladky said the *Gazette* initially used Olive software that allows the entire newspaper, including ads, to be put on the website. That software was upgraded to Technavia in 2006. Readers can click on an ad or story to bring it up on the screen. If a store has a link on the page, readers can click on the link, buy whatever is shown online, and come back to the *Gazette* home page and continue reading.

One of the biggest advantages of the new technology is that it makes the company a twenty-four-hour news source. But does it detract from the newspaper? Hladky said he doesn't know. Alluding to the company mission statement, he said, "It said we're going to be an information provider of choice through a dynamic mix of products and services. It doesn't say we're a newspaper. It doesn't say we're a television station. It doesn't say we are an Internet site." That mindset shows the company is consumer oriented, not product oriented. "It said, 'Mr. and Mrs. Consumer, if you want information, we want you coming to our company' rather than 'You have to buy the newspaper' or 'You have to watch Channel 9.' And ironically the statement was written before the Internet. For a long time, we have known the Internet was coming, but we didn't know what it would become," he said.

"I would maintain that there is no organization in eastern Iowa that knows more about eastern Iowa than we do. And if we can't turn that ability to gather information to edit and to put a product in print, in cyberspace, on TV, on radio; if we can't take that information and mine the area where we have reporters and contacts and understanding; if we can't turn that into a buck, shame on us. Then we'll have to sell."[25]

Circulation Issues

Being locally owned has helped Swenson cope with changes in circulation practices. Circulation systems are getting more sophisticated every year, but they require big capital investments that cannot be spread out over several properties if a paper is locally owned. A knowledge base that is confined to one property can be another disadvantage. "There's not a lot of ideas coming out unless we venture outside our walls," he said, "which means we need to put considerable effort into partnerships and information exchanges and probably a greater-than-normal investment in things like conferences so that we can keep up with what's going in the world, especially being in the Midwest."

The *Gazette* does not have what some theorists call ego circulation, or distribution to areas that cost more than the revenue they bring in. "We scrutinize every single area. We're looking for a profit or cash flow contribution from every paper that we're delivering, so any areas that were marginal for us, we trimmed back a little bit," he said. In some rural areas where there were only a few newspapers in a community, subscribers were converted to mail subscriptions. "But we do have an extremely large footprint, and the footprint we have for delivery is all profitable," Swenson said. "We focus strictly on top-line circulation. So we're looking at everything that would be considered in the category of 50 percent or greater. And we've actually got less than 2 percent of our circulation that's in the below-twenty-five-paid category, the bulk of that being Newspapers in Education. So we really don't focus on some of the promotional games that you can play with circulation. We strictly keep focused on customers and readers that provide value to advertisers and the company."

The *Gazette* has seen some circulation declines, but Swenson said circulation cash flow has actually increased over the last couple of years, and the number of core subscribers (those customers who have been with the *Gazette* for more than a year) is increasing. He said in the past the company used a number of independent distributors, but they dissolved many of those relationships and have gone to direct management, thus expanding their employee base. "By doing that, we find a lot of efficiencies that those independent contractors just can't realize," he said. "There's insurance cost, bookkeeping cost and assistants, and all those types of things that, whether you have three hundred carriers or six hundred carriers, we have the same amount of overhead." So the *Gazette* overhauled its distribution structure from one where bundles were dropped for the carriers to one that uses centralized distribution centers. "We've been able to reduce our trucking costs as a result of that, which in turn, makes us a little less susceptible to the fuel costs." But despite those changes, the *Gazette* still has about eight thousand miles of daily travel with carriers and relay trucks. When fuel prices rose, the company instituted subsidies to reflect the actual cost of the carriers and the drivers to operate. As fuel prices eased, that expense went away. "The way we handled it financially was that when the market was in the jitters like that, when fuel costs were way up, they weren't responding to marketing pieces, so we pulled back on our direct mail for a couple of months," Swenson said. "We took that money and moved it over to the subsidizing, said we're going to maintain our customer base and quality of service, and now we're starting to reenergize the marketing efforts again." The key to coping with market fluctuations is budget flexibility, a huge plus for family owned newspapers.

When Do-Not-Call lists undermined telemarketing, the *Gazette* suffered like many businesses. Historically about two-thirds of new subscriptions came from telemarketing, Swenson said. But now "we're diversifying. We've put a lot more effort into retaining customers and really being focused on that first six months of a new subscriber." He describes twelve touch points that have been identified in that first six months for new customers. "We've created a welcome kit. We've assigned each new customer their own customer service representative as a personal touch. And that person is checking up on that customer periodically, making sure their delivery started OK, that they were happy with the service, and if they have any questions about the product and how they might navigate it." There is also a rewards program on the customer's first renewal, personalized direct-mail efforts rather than mass marketing, and identifying target groups. "It's not a one-size-fits-all approach anymore," he said.

One strategy for the future is to acquire new single-copy buyers before they become home-delivery buyers. "People aren't going to just jump from being a nonreader into being a subscriber," Swenson said. "We need to get them buying at the newsstand, maybe for a period of years. So we've started efforts to try and do some sampling with single copy and just get the newspaper into people's hands. Things like pass-along copies at the office may be working in our favor instead of against us like we used to think in the past."

Customer service drives the *Gazette* Circulation Department. Carriers deliver to the porch, and the company promotes porching the paper as a customer service. "We're committed to porch delivery," Swenson said. "I kind of have the philosophy that we need to provide great service to everyone rather than exceptional service to a few." If customers have a history of getting the newspaper delivered to the back door, even between the door and the screen, "we'll maintain that as long as we can, but we're not setting up any new ones that way. All the new ones are set up to be porch delivery or tube delivery if it's a rural area." Service levels continue to improve partly because considerable effort has been put into training field workers to understand how the paper is received rather than how it is delivered. Single-bagging and tossing it onto a driveway, leads to pinholes and wet papers if it rains. "When we made the conversion to distribution centers, that helped tremendously," Swenson said. There used to be a shortage driver operation that would kick in if a subscriber was missed or had a wet paper. There was another person ready to be dispatched to take a new one to them. "That was a separate group than the people that were supervising the carriers," he said. But "when we went to the distribution centers, the people that are supervising the carriers also become responsible for the make-goods, and once the problem fell into their laps, it cut it by three-fourth." It is the carriers' decision to bag the paper, but the Circulation Department strongly encourages it. "We're looking at making the bag part of the newspaper and not being an option," he said.

The distribution centers are based on team management. There are about one hundred carriers who come to each distribution center where there are three to four district managers and a coordinator or shopkeeper who opens and closes the center and doles out the inventory to the carriers. The team approach has improved employee satisfaction, productivity, and recruitment, Swenson said. "That was driven by making more efficient decisions," he said. "We wanted frontline decisions rather than running things up the management ladder, and we thought it would give us greater customer satisfaction if we just took care of problems immediately."

More than 99 percent of the *Gazette*'s subscriptions are paid in advance through the office or with a credit card. All promotional efforts are geared toward prepay. "We have almost no bad debt. It's just not an issue for us," Swenson said.[26]

The Future

Bowden said he still sees a future for a print version of the newspaper, but it will continue to evolve in format, shape, and size. Newspapers will look at the costs of production and may change as magazines have over the years. "But as far as it being a purveyor of information, an institution that sells information, we're here to stay," he said. A company like the *Gazette* isn't solely a distributor of information. "We're selling information to people who want it," he said, "and we're trying to make sure that we can give people the choice, which heretofore was just impossible." Two staffers are dedicated to putting out the e-edition of the newspaper, and they are breaking news online. Reporters cover a story in the morning and write a version first for the online edition, which is updated as many times during the day as needed.[27]

Peters said he is motivated by a desire to develop the information provider for the future. He said he believes the company should not focus on the distribution medium but rather the core process they are engaged in—"aggregating and editing and disseminating primarily local information." But the operation has to be efficient. Peters was hired to implement a company restructuring several years ago and successfully combined seven operating units into three. He recognizes that the industry is going through an enormous transition, but he is motivated to see it through. "The strength of the company is our relationship with the community, our reputation for being accurate and timely and relevant and balanced, including the relationship with the local advertisers ...," he said. "If we distribute that through paper today and we end up distributing it online tomorrow or some other method of distribution, that's not really important."

Peters will not commit to online being the future of the company, and he said he is not ready to accept the pronouncement that newspapers are dead. One of the people who declared newspapers dead was Bill Gates, Microsoft founder, who later acknowledged he was wrong. Peters said there is an old argument "about the chair or the screen." Reading on a computer is not a pleasant experience for many reasons, he said, whether it is on a cell phone, a laptop, or a PDA. He said work is under way to improve online text to make it more readable on the screen. "We're going to have better resolution. We're going to have more flexibility," he said. One innovation is e-ink that uses a flexible piece of material that simulates the same experience as actually reading the newspaper. Instead of flipping a page, however, the reader presses the corner. Peters said there are two types of e-inks under development. "One involves little spheres that are turned certain ways depending on certain electrical charges, so what you do instead of having a newspaper printed and delivered to you is you plug it into the Internet or whatever. In the middle of the night, your piece of plastic changes, and there's enough memory in a chip that you can hold a whole newspaper. There is a little switch that lets you flip the pages. You can still have the experience, but you don't have the distribution issues."[28]

Niche publications, commercial printing, blogging, exploring "interactive opportunities where people can interact with the news" are focuses of *Gazette* research and development, Schmitz said. "I think the idea that the *Gazette* has done the research and has presented the news, no matter what it's on, is going to have value," she said. "I don't know what that younger generation is going to bring, and I may be deluding myself, but I think that's going to have value because it's an entity. It's an independent source that has been providing news for a number of years. And if they provide it via Internet, via pushing it out to your cell phone, or what have you, it's still that credibility of the brand that people understand where it's coming from. ... I think that has value. How to get it out to people and maintain that value, that's going to be a challenge"[29]

Swenson said success in the future is based on the company's ability to innovate. "What we've done in the past has no value, really to our success in the future," he said. It is important to keep trying new things. The key is to always look to change, "especially now that we know that the print world has a predictable future. There's going to be a slow, steady decline in the print world for years to come, so we have to be building up another venue to shape our future. That said, print is going to be viable for a long, long time.

"More niche applications, more responsiveness to readers' needs—maybe even less information. We always add and add and add, and with the time-value equation today, more isn't always better. So maybe doing less would add more value to the time of our readers. We have to be really scrupulous about what we publish."[30]

Hladky has the last word: "Our ownership has always supported efforts to expand into other services as we try to grow the value of the company. Initially it was broadcast. Later we invested in a Yellow Page company, *Iowa Farmer Today*; the Breakthrough reading program, Decisionmark; and many other ventures outside of our core media business. I really appreciate the confidence our ownership has had in management since I was given the stewardship of the Gazette Company. Our goal has, and always will be, to keep growing the business that was started by C. L. Miller and Fred Faulkes."[31]

In February 2009, the Gazette Company announced it would cut one hundred jobs as part of a company-wide reorganization, the Associated Press reported. In the story, Peters blamed the worsening economy, rising newsprint costs, and floods that swept the area in summer 2008, affecting many of the company's advertisers. The staff cuts would leave the company with about five hundred employees, Peters said.[32] Bowden left the newspaper in December 2007, and Steve Buttry, formerly of the American Press Institute, replaced him the following June.[33]

Notes

1   Joe Hladky (chairman, Gazette Company), interview with the author, Dec. 1, 2005.
2   Joe Hladky, *The Enduring Vision: The Gazette Co.* (Cedar Rapids: Gazette Co., 2005), 57.
3   Joe Hladky, interview.
4   *The Enduring Vision*, 13.
5   http://www.gazetteonline.com/.
6   Joe Hladky, interview.
7   *The Enduring Vision*, 47.
8   Peg Schmitz (general manager and vice president of operations, the *Gazette* in Cedar Rapids), interview with the author, Dec. 1, 2005.
9   *The Enduring Vision*, 16.
10 Ibid., 57.
11 Chuck Peters (president and chief executive officer, the *Gazette* in Cedar Rapids), interview with the author, Dec. 1, 2005.
12 *The Enduring Vision*, 52–53.
13 Elizabeth Hladky (home delivery manager, the *Gazette* in Cedar Rapids), interview with the author, Dec. 1, 2005.
14 *The Enduring Vision*, 53.
15 Elizabeth Hladky, interview.
16 *The Enduring Vision*, 2–3.
17 Joe Hladky, interview.
18 *The Enduring Vision*, 54–56.
19 Mark Bowden (former editor, the *Gazette* in Cedar Rapids), interview with the author, Dec. 1, 2005.
20 Joe Hladky, interview.
21 Schmitz, interview.
22 Scott Swenson (circulation director, the *Gazette* in Cedar Rapids), interview with the author, Dec. 1, 2005.
23 Bowden, interview.
24 http://gazetteonline.com/faq/#faq4.
25 Joe Hladky, interview.
26 Swenson, interview.
27 Bowden, interview.
28 Peters, interview.
29 Schmitz, interview.
30 Swenson, interview.
31 *The Enduring Vision*, 91.
32 Associated Press, "The Gazette Company announces restructuring," Feb. 25, 2009, http://www.kttc.com/Global/story.asp?s=9902594&clienttype=printable.
33 http://www.poynter.org/column.asp?id=45&aid=142808.

A Final Word

While American newspapers are busy covering world and domestic disasters, war and politics, and the challenges of businesses in an uncertain world, one important story on the minds of many journalists, industry analysts, and academics is whether newspapers, themselves, can survive in today's crushing climate of corporate journalism. Articles are written frequently questioning the future of newspapers and predicting that the continued slide in advertising dollars, rising production costs, threat of the Internet as a news source, and pressures from Wall Street will bring the demise of what many analysts call a mature industry. It is time for further examination of an ownership model that can take newspaper companies through these troubled times.

In 2006, the number of daily newspapers in the United States declined 23 percent since 1940, and in 2007 there was a further loss of 1 percent.[1] Part of that decrease is linked to a trend in American business in the last fifty years for companies to go from private ownership to ownership by investors. In the mid-twentieth century, individuals or families owned most newspapers. Today, chains own a majority.

When newspaper companies started going public in the 1960s, many that had been driven for decades by a long-term commitment to their communities and excellence in journalism found themselves controlled by Wall Street expectations of increasing profitability and high shareholder return. The result, argues Philip Meyer in *The Vanishing Newspaper*, coupled with new technologies and declining readership and confidence, has left an industry "in peril."[2]

But what about the newspapers left that are locally owned and have been in a family for generations? Are their business models so different that they have a better chance of surviving and thriving?

The underlying question then is what makes family owned newspapers different from those owned by public companies? To answer this, a case-study approach was used to examine eight family owned newspapers, large and small, and in different regions of the country. The case studies describe the companies' operations and why family ownership may put them at an advantage over their publicly owned peers. In-depth interviews were conducted with the newspapers' publishers, top managers, and others who could define their business strategy and daily operations. The case studies document the story of these newspapers as the first decade of the twenty-first century draws to a close. The findings suggest that the family owned newspaper model may give them a brighter future because they can play by different rules.

The Positives and the Negatives

Family owned newspaper companies are decidedly different from their publicly owned counterparts. The following are positive factors about family owned newspaper companies that all of the newspapers in the case studies have in common:

- They have functional autonomy, can set their own agendas, and can focus on a long-range plan rather than short-term financial results.
- They have streamlined operations and the ability to make quick decisions about their business and news coverage.
- They are not driven by Wall Street, public stockholders, or the bottom line.
- They have long-term relationships with local advertisers and other family businesses.
- They have strong family pride and a strong sense of their role in their communities.
- They have more control over ad rates, staff size, and profit margin.
- They have a strong and loyal readership base made up of generations of readers who trust the newspaper.

They aren't a utopia, though. Some families own newspapers solely to make money or for the notoriety that comes with owning a city's newspaper. Some also use their influence for personal gain.

But family owned newspaper companies do face special challenges. The following are negative factors found at family owned newspapers:

- They have limited resources.
- They lack strong corporate backing.
- They have limited support services.
- They oftentimes lack succession planning.
- They sometimes are too close to their communities.
- They often are engaged in family squabbles.
- They can lack company diversity.

All of these factors can impede family owned businesses' success, and some of them can derail companies, specifically a lack of succession planning and family squabbles. One family newspaper expert, John Mennenga, facilitator of the Independent Newspaper Group, said he believes family owned newspapers could have a brighter future than publicly owned ones if the family members can continue to get along.[3]

Why Should We Care?

Because newspapers are an essential element in a democracy, their future is vital to the success of public life. Even evolving technologies and changes in social practices haven't diminished the importance of the public's need for information and a forum to discuss it. Family owned newspapers can better fulfill the public's needs and those of a democracy because they are fundamentally different operationally and philosophically from those that are publicly owned.

Ultimately, the future of any newspaper is largely dependent on its owners' priorities, their satisfaction level, and the site of the center of power. Regardless of whether a newspaper is owned by a public or private company, a family or an investment group, if owners increasingly demand higher earnings, operational strategies shift from focusing on delivering quality journalism to delivering higher profits. And there is a tipping point where this shift in priorities erodes the newspaper's business, product, and value. Local autonomy—the ability to make decisions at the local level that drive the business—as well as the owner's satisfaction or at least willingness to accept financial returns, priorities, and commitment to the core business of journalism enhance the newspaper's future.

As publicly owned newspaper companies continue to decline in today's fiercely challenging economic environment, there could be more ownership changes in the future. The sale of Knight Ridder, the Tribune Company, and Dow Jones in 2006 and 2007 shocked the industry. There were further extreme events at newspapers in 2008 and 2009, including Chapter 11 bankruptcy filings, shutdowns, moving to online publication only, and ending delivery of print editions on some days of the week. As revenues continued to decline and the recession deepened, most companies were forced to implement cost-cutting strategies that included staff and pay cuts, salary freezes, mandatory furloughs, decreases in the news hole and the physical size of the newspaper, and cutting back on distribution.[4]

What Family Newspaper Owners Need to Do

(Based on case studies of eight family owned newspaper companies)

- Avoid family squabbles. This is critical and among the highest priorities. Appointing outside members to the board can lend an independent voice and ease family negotiations.

- Develop a strong succession plan. You must have someone interested and ready to step into a leadership role, but of course he or she doesn't have to be a family member.

- Groom your next generation for the business, give them plenty of opportunity to gain a variety of experience at the company, and listen to their fresh ideas.

- Invest in research and development. Newspapers don't do much of this, but they should. Most other successful businesses do.

- Carefully calculate the benefits and costs of new product development. Trusted outside advisers can help determine if the company's financials can support a new venture.

- Search for new business opportunities and ways to diversity your company. Different businesses have different business cycles that compliment one another in successful companies.

- Network with other family newspaper owners. Share information, experiences, and advice in pursuit of common goals.

- Innovate by using new technology. This requires a great deal of collaboration with experts and others.

- Stay flexible in decision making. Make thoughtful decisions on operations, but if they don't work, don't be afraid to change the plan.

- Keep a budget and keep to the budget. Manage the company with strong financial discipline but with compassion.

- Streamline operations. Keep the staff you need but not more than you need.

- Focus on the long-term, but keep the short-term numbers in mind. You must plan for your company's future and how you will get there.

- Build loyalty in your staff. Family newspapers generally have strong staff loyalty. There is little loyalty to owners at public newspapers. This makes family newspapers different, so capitalize on it.

- Balance good journalism with good business. Both are equally important, and you don't have to choose one over the other.

- Stay true to the principles of journalism. It should be why you are in the business.

- Cherish your family legacy. Realize you are in the business of journalism, not just newspapers, and it is a great business to be in.
- Stay passionate and embrace change. You have a long history of success behind you.

While not immune to the same economic pressures all newspaper companies face today, family ownership may prove to be a better and more sustainable business model because power rests not in outside investors but in the smaller group of owners. That local center of power will continue to drive decisions that better position these newspapers to meet the external challenges they face from falling ad revenue, higher production costs, changing readership habits, and new technology. And it will allow newspapers to strategically meet the challenges of economic fluctuations without outside influence. Family owned newspapers simply have more control over their reactions to tough times.

The era of newspaper consolidation seems to be over, after the trend toward public ownership obsessed with successive quarters of higher profits spiraled out of control. The new trend for the future could be smaller, independent newspaper companies run by families or small groups of private investors who, one can only hope, return their focus to the core business of journalism. Newspapers unquestionably will look and be different in the future, and the surviving ones will be those enhanced by opportunities arising from technological innovation. Change is a part of the long, storied history of newspapers, and so is adaptation. Newspapers, especially family owned ones, have shown that they are masters at innovation and navigating change.

Notes

1 The Pew Research Center's Project for Excellence in Journalism, The State of the News Media 2009, http://www.stateofthemedia.org/2009/narrative_newspapers_audience.php?media=4&cat=2.
2 Philip Meyer, *The Vanishing Newspaper: Saving Journalism in the Information Age*, (Columbia: University of Missouri Press, 2004), 10.
3 John Mennenga (Independent Newspaper Group), interview with the author, July 24, 2007.
4 The Pew Research Center's Project for Excellence in Journalism, The State of the News Media 2009, http://www.stateofthemedia.org/2009/narrative_newspapers_economics.php?media=4&cat=3.

Bibliography

Arkansas Gazette Company v. Camden News Publishing Company, No. LR C 84 1020 (E.D. Ark. 1986), Defendant's Trial Exhibit # 548.

———, Defendant's Trial Exhibit # 596.

———, Defendant's Trial Exhibit # 602.

Bowden, William. "Northwest Arkansas Newspapers at War." Master's thesis, University of Arkansas, 1998.

Fitzgerald, Mark. "The key to victory: Publisher tells how his Arkansas Democrat prevailed in the brutal Little Rock newspaper war; cites competitor's blunder." *Editor & Publisher* (March 28, 1992): 17.

———. "A veil of secrecy: Rumors suggest end to Little Rock newspaper war." *Editor & Publisher* (Oct. 5, 1991): 35.

Hladky, Joe. *The Enduring Vision: The Gazette Co.* Cedar Rapids: the Gazette Co., 2005: 2–91.

Kovach, Bill and Tom Rosenstiel. *The Elements of Journalism.* New York: Three Rivers Press, 2001: 17.

Mencher, Melvin. *News Reporting and Writing.* New York: McGraw-Hill, 2011: 69.

Meyer, Philip. *The Vanishing Newspaper: Saving Journalism in the Information Age.* Columbia: University of Missouri Press, 2004: 10.

Overholser, Geneva. "Editor Inc." In Roberts, *Leaving Readers Behind: The Age of Corporate Newspapering*, 174.

Pearce, Charles W. "They Both Bled Red, The Little Rock Newspaper War." Master's thesis, University of Arkansas, 2000.

Reed, Roy. "Giant," In Roberts, *Leaving Readers Behind: The Age of Corporate Newspapering*, 303.

Risser, James V. "Independent Papers: An Endangered Species." In Roberts, *Leaving Readers Behind: The Age of Corporate Newspapering*, 394–395.

Roberts, Gene. "Leaving Readers Behind." In Roberts, *Leaving Readers Behind: The Age of Corporate Newspapering*, 15.

———, ed. *Leaving Readers Behind: The Age of Corporate Newspapering.* Fayetteville: University of Arkansas Press, 2001.

Walton, Mary. "The Selling of Small-Town America," In Roberts, *Leaving Readers Behind: The Age of Corporate Newspapering*, 51.

Index